A C

I have endeavoured in
this Ghostly little book,
to raise the Ghost of
an Idea, which shall
not put my readers
out of humour with
themselves, with
each other, with the
season, or with me.
May it haunt their
houses pleasantly . . .

Charles Dickens, December 1843

Charles Dickens' *A Christmas Carol*, published in 1843, is one of the best-loved stories to be set at this time of year. The story has been adapted into many films, and is such a powerful tale that it's credited with helping to define our contemporary understanding of Christmas.

But a fresh look at this all-time classic, reminds us that it's far more than just a feel-good festive tale featuring a miserly old humbug. In fact, the story of Ebenezer Scrooge and his tormenting spirits helps us to consider what is of eternal value today.

Dickens set out to persuade his readers to summon the spirit of Christmas not just at Christmas, but also for all the year. His message has a timeless, universal quality, like all the best works of art.

The book's main character is the mean and intimidating Ebenezer Scrooge, who lives to make money and very little else. He certainly has no use for religion or sentimentality.

One Christmas Eve, however, Scrooge receives a terrifying wake-up call. The spirit of his business partner, Jacob Marley, who died seven Christmas Eves previous, comes to visit, bound and wrapped in heavy chains. Marley has been condemned to roam the face of the earth, tormented in death by the things he neglected to value in life.

He is desperate to give his old colleague a final chance to avoid the same fate. 'My spirit never walked beyond our counting-house,' he warns Scrooge. 'My spirit never roved beyond the narrow limits of our money-changing hole . . .' This, he makes clear, is

Scrooge's last opportunity to turn from his selfish and insular ways. Marley's spirit instructs him to wait for three more spirits of Christmas past, present and future. Reluctantly, Scrooge understands that this is for real, as he sees Marley float away to join a crowd of tormented souls who are wailing and moaning in the night sky.

On the stroke of one o'clock, the Spirit of Christmas Past arrives, and takes him on an unforgettable trip down memory lane, on a visit to his own childhood.

Scrooge is astonished to see old, familiar faces playing happily in the open air. As the Spirit takes him into a schoolroom, however, they see a lonely little boy sitting by the fire, whose only companion is the book he is reading.

Scrooge remembers his loneliness, and how he longed for the presence and warmth of friends. He recalls his past desires for the love and approval of his family, but then sees all the people who tried to reach out to him, who attempted to stop his slide into self-absorption and an increasing preoccupation with personal security.

He sees his former fiancée, Belle, who came a poor second to Scrooge's passion for wealth. 'A golden idol displaces me,' she complains to him from the past. 'All hopes have merged to a master passion; the thought of money engrosses you!'

Dickens explores, through Scrooge's terrifying ordeal, the love of money compared with the value of relationships. Scrooge's whole life has come to revolve around his counting-house. His insatiable appetite consumes him for more. To him, Christmas has become nothing more than a 'time for finding yourself a year older, but not an hour richer'.

Today, in the 21st century, we can fall into a similar trap, seeing money – and the things it can buy – as the answer to our problems, especially if our lives have not been that happy, like the young Ebenezer Scrooge's. We perceive the 'good life' as being about an abundance of bigger, brighter and better things.

Jacob Marley's ghostly visit is not just a wake-up call for Scrooge. As we hear his words, we should make sure we haven't lost out on the things that money can't buy. We all need money, of course, but it's possible to pay too high a price for it. It's as if society has caught a cultural disease called 'affluenza'. The symptoms include always wanting more, despite what we already have. And then there's the insatiable desire for 'success' without experiencing contentment. Consistently, we choose our career over family. And we seem unwilling to settle for less than the best of everything.

The Second Spirit

If Scrooge has been shaken by the visit of the first spirit, then the second is no less disturbing. The Spirit of Christmas Present arrives to take Scrooge on a tour of the people he now knows. He finds himself standing in the home of his poor clerk, Bob Cratchit, where he feels the warmth of a large and friendly family who are making the best of what little they can afford on the tiny salary Scrooge pays. He experiences their anxiety over the fate of Tiny Tim, the Cratchits' sick, youngest child.

Scrooge is clearly shown the effects of his selfish nature; but the Spirit helps him understand that even though he is utterly hard-hearted, others have not entirely given up on him. As they sit down to their feeble Christmas dinner, Bob Cratchit thinks to toast his employer, despite protests from his wife.

The Spirit of Christmas Present then shows Scrooge the harsh reality of life on the streets, together with the absolute determination of the families who live there to stay out of the prisons

and workhouses, whatever the cost. Scrooge has never before seen the need to help anyone other than himself. He's always believed that the poor should go to the institutions provided – 'If they would rather die, they had better do it, and decrease the surplus population.'

Then, the Spirit reveals two hauntingly thin and deathly children from within his cloak. They are called IGNORANCE and WANT – two of the grim realities of Victorian life. The Spirit describes them as the 'children of all who walk the earth unseen'. On their brow is written 'DOOM'.

But it is not the quivering, hollow children who are doomed. As Scrooge pleads for them to be removed from his sight, the Spirit explains that ignorance and want 'spells the downfall of you and all those who deny their existence'.

Before you put someone in his or her place, you should put yourself in his or hers. How much poverty do we allow ourselves to see? The Spirit responds, 'They are hidden, but they live.' Dickens holds a mirror not just to Scrooge's face, but also to ours. How do we treat the poor, the weak and the vulnerable? Do we shield ourselves from the needs of the poor and downtrodden?

After all, we are not on this earth to see through one another, but to see one another through.

The Final Spirit

Then comes the final spirit, the Spirit of Christmas Future, who has no face and does not speak. It merely points. Scrooge looks to where the Spirit is leading him, and sees the Cratchit family again, worn down in their struggle against poverty, and now without Tiny Tim, who has died for lack of proper medical care.

The Spirit takes Scrooge to visit the house of a man who has died in his sleep. A maid and a cleaner are dividing up his belongings before the undertaker arrives. Two associates are discussing whether it's even necessary to hold a funeral service, since no one would bother to come.

'But who is this man?' asks Scrooge. The Spirit leads him to a grave, whose headstone bears the name 'Ebenezer Scrooge'. It's a chilling reminder that no one lives forever; that the journey of life is brief. As the Bible says, 'our days on earth are like a shadow' (1 Chronicles 29:15, NIV).

This is the life-changing moment when Scrooge understands that it's now or never. He asks whether it's possible to mend his ways and so alter his life and destiny. Surely the Spirits wouldn't be visiting him if not? As Christmas morning dawns and he wakes, once more, to the world, Scrooge realises that he has been given a reprieve. He has another chance to be more human – just as Dickens believed we have all been given another opportunity, because of the birth of Jesus Christ.

RIP

EBENEZER
SCROOGE

Many of us will recognise the struggles of Ebenezer Scrooge in our own lives. Many of us have been hurt as we grew up. Many of us pass up the offer of friendship or kindness out of a fear of rejection. Scrooge was a man who lived in a prison of his own making, the doors shut and sealed with a bitterness which he would not let go.

In fact, Dickens symbolises the consequence of our selfish actions by the chain that traps Jacob Marley's spirit and weighs him down. Marley tells Scrooge that he alone forged it in life: 'I made it link by link, and yard by yard.'

His chains were forged with regrets, which he could not release, and hurts he would not forgive. And as he stands before Scrooge, he can see the even greater chains that bind his old colleague: 'Would you know the weight and length of the strong coil you bear yourself?' asks Marley. 'It was full as heavy and as long as this, seven Christmas Eves ago. You have laboured on it since. It is a ponderous chain!'

The good news is that we can learn from the past, to change now so that we can create a better future. Just as the Spirits of Christmas wanted Scrooge to change for good, so God knows us better than we know ourselves, and loves us enough to help us to change and make a difference.

Christmas is the time and place where God draws back the curtain so we can see his face. Jesus has come to free us, because we are bound by chains. In fact, because of Jesus, we can commemorate the past, consecrate the present and contemplate the future. Jesus came to give us a new outlook on life.

The good news is that we, like Scrooge, are still alive. It's not too late: we can choose to change. Life can only be understood backwards, but it must be lived forwards. Whatever our past has been, we can have a better future.

At the heart of *A Christmas Carol* lies Scrooge's transformation. From a selfish, greedy and bitter old man, we see him become a grateful, generous and compassionate figure. A man filled with deep regret sees his life transformed, to the point where Dickens concludes 'he became as good a friend, as good a master, and as good a man, as the good old city knew'.

Things do not change. We do. Scrooge learns his lesson, and experiences what amounts to a 'conversion'. He responds by changing his ways and living out the lessons that he learnt on

that Christmas Eve. He repents and changes his destiny.

Jesus, the Son of God, invites us to do the same. What better time than Christmas to receive forgiveness, renew our faith, release our fears and rebuild our friendships?

In case you are still making a Christmas list, here are some timeless gifts that won't cost you anything except, perhaps, a little pride. You could mend a quarrel, release a grudge, lessen your demands on others, apologise, forgive someone who has treated you wrongly, find a forgotten friend, write an overdue thank-you note, point out one thing you appreciate most about someone you live with or work with, tell someone you love them, or give something away.

You cannot do a kindness too soon, because you never know how soon it will be too late.

We talk about 'the birth of new ideas' and of hope being 'born' in the human heart. Why not let Jesus be born into your life, this Christmas time? It takes a conscious, personal decision to become a follower of Jesus, which begins by acknowledging that we all need him – to forgive us for what we have done wrong, and to guide us into *real* life, the life he promised to give us 'to the full' by his Holy Spirit and experience a dynamic, living relationship with God our creator – is surely worth it.

If you want to make this Christmas one to remember, then there's no need to wait any longer. If you ask Jesus to forgive your past, and invite him to enter your Christmas present, then your life will be transformed – now, and for good.

Dickens sent a message to us in the form of an amazing story. God sends his message in the form of his Son, Jesus Christ, who lives today. In the words of the wonderful carol 'O Little Town of Bethlehem', we can invite Jesus to be with us, like he was, all those years ago at the first Christmas:

O holy Child of Bethlehem, descend to us, we pray;

Cast out our sin, and enter in, be born in us today.

We hear the Christmas angels the great glad tidings tell;

O come to us, abide with us, our Lord Emmanuel!

May God grant you the light
of Christmas, which is faith;

The warmth of Christmas,
which is love;

The radiance of Christmas,
which is purity;

The righteousness of
Christmas, which is justice;

The belief in Christmas,
which is truth;

The all of Christmas,
which is Christ.

As we celebrate the birth of Jesus, may
God grant you all these things – not just
at Christmas, but also throughout the
New Year and all the years to come.

THE
HINDU ART OF LOVE

G000022396

THE
HINDU ART OF LOVE

Translated by
Sir Richard F. Burton

PILGRIMS PUBLISHING
Varanasi♦Kathmandu

THE HINDU ART OF LOVE
Translated by Sir Richard F. Burton

Published by:
PILGRIMS PUBLISHING

An imprint of:
PILGRIMS BOOK HOUSE
B 27/98 A-8, Nawabganj Road
Durga Kund
Varanasi, India 221010
Telephone: 91-542-314060, 312456, 312496
Fax: 91-542-314059
E-mail: pilgrims@satyam.net.in

Distributed in India by:
BOOK FAITH INDIA
414-416 Express Tower
Azadpur Commercial Complex
New Delhi-110033, India
Tel: 91-11-713-2459
Fax: 91-11-724-9674
E-mail: pilgrim@del2.vsnl.net.in

Distributed in Nepal by:
PILGRIMS BOOK HOUSE
P.O Box 3872
Kathmandu, Nepal
Fax: 977-1-424943
E-mail: pilgrims@wlink.com.np

First published in by
Castle Books, New York

Copyright © 2000, Pilgrims Publishing
All Rights Reserved

ISBN 81-7769-002-7

Cover design by Sasya

Printed in India

Introduction to the New Edition

Sir Richard Burton started his career with the East India Company in 1842 and during his tenure developed a thorough knowledge of Persian, Afghan, Hindustani and Arabic. A widely traveled and well read person he went on to document his many journeys and adventures. Amongst his most famous journeys are his clandestine visit to Medina and Mecca followed by his search for the source of the Nile. After an adventurous and eventful life he devoted his last years to literature

He was a translator of extraordinary virtuosity. Amongst his works are translations of the six volumes of Camoes, a volume of Neapolitan Italian tales by Giambattista Basile, Il Pentamarona and Latin poems by Catullus. What excited him most was the erotica of the East. He took it upon himself to introduce the West to the sexual wisdom of the ancient Eastern manuals on the art of love. To do this he personally faced prosecution and secretly published the Kama Sutra of Vatsyayana (1853), and The Perfumed Gardens of the Sheik Nefzaoui. He also translated and published openly an unexpurgated version of the Arabian Nights (1885-1888) which was so exceptional for its fidelity, masculine vigour, and literary skill that it frightened away all competitors.

The present translation by Sir Richard Burton of Ananga Ranga (1885) is not for the philanderer but more for those who wish to make a success of their marriage. It was written to promote complete physical enjoyment in married life. This book unlike the *Kama Sutra* of Vatsayana does not go into the art of making love. Rather it is more concerned with the development of the relations between a husband and wife until each one fully satisfies the other. Thus, it in fact discourages a polygamous relationship in the guise of marriage and removes the causes of unnecessary confusions, which may arise from such a situation.

This book is most relevant in this age of recognised promiscuity when even in India divorce and separation in certain segments of society has become recognised as a necessary evil to maintain social order and decorum. The book rightly points out that the relationship between a man and his wife is much of their own making. It shows how each of the partners may develop a harmonious and happy scenario in their own lives and may cause their relationship to be one of complete satisfaction both physically and mentally, notwithstanding the shortcomings either may have.

One might say that this book is an extension of the *Kama Sutra* where one may progress from the actual conquest to the actual settlement and enjoyment of one's married life. Marital conjugality is a perennial and common problem faced by all at some stage in their lives. It has been pointed out in this book that it mainly depends upon the behaviour of the married couple themselves, for it must be assumed that once one is sexually satisfied, mental satisfaction is not far behind. If this aspect is taken care of, other facets of married life fall into place without too much effort. Probably incompatibility in the bedroom has led to the break-up of more marriages than say infidelity, which is usually the end result in such situations.

This is a book to be read and understood thoroughly and then put into practice. It is one which should be treasured and re-read from time to time. The result would lead to more successful and satisfying marriages.

C.N. Burchett
Varanasi
April, 2000

CONTENTS

INTRODUCTION

MAY you be purified by Parvati[1] who coloured the nails
of her hands, which were white like the waters of

[1] The mountain-goddess of many names, wife of Shiva, the third
person of the Hindu Trinity, who is here termed Shambhu for Sway-
ambhu, the Self-Existent. The invocation is abrupt and does not
begin with the beginning, Ganesha (Janus), Lord of Incepts, who is
invariably invoked by the Hindu, that he may further the new
undertaking. This god is worshipped under the form of a short stout
man, with an elephant's trunk and protuberant belly. (See Vol. III,
p. 38, "A View of the History, Literature, and Mythology of the
Hindus," by William Ward, of Serampore, London, 1832.) The loves
of Krishna and the sixteen thousand milkmaids are recorded in the
Bhagavat; this eleventh incarnation of Vishnu is a dark-blue man,
playing with both hands upon the pipe, whilst Radha, his wife, stands
on his left side. Kamadeva, or the Hindu Cupid, the son of Bramha,
is represented as a beautiful youth, the most lovely of all the gods,
holding a bow and flower-tipped arrow, with which, while wandering
through perfumed glades, accompanied by Rati, his spouse, he wounds
the hearts of the inhabitants of the Triloka or Three Worlds. Sir
William Jones says that he appears to correspond with the Greek Eros
and the Roman Cupido, but that the Indian description of his person
and arms, his family, attendants and attributes has new and peculiar
beauties. Sambar' A'sura was one of the Rakshasas, gigantic and
diabolical beings, whom Kama slew.

Ganges, with lac after seeing the fire on the forehead of Shambhu; who painted her eyes with collyrium after seeing the dark hues of Shambhu's neck and whose body-hair stood erect (with desire) after seeing in a mirror the ashes on Shambhu's body.

I invoke thee, O Kamadeva! thee the sportive; thee, the wanton one, who dwellest in the hearts of all created beings;

Thou instillest courage in time of war; thou destroyedst Sambar' A'sura and the Rakshasas; thou sufficest unto Rati[2], and to the loves and pleasures of the world;

Thou art ever cheerful, removing uneasiness and over-activity, and thou givest comfort and happiness to the mind of man.

King Ahmad was the ornament of the Lodi House. He was a Sea, having for waters the tears shed by the widows of his slaughtered foes, and he rose to just renown and wide-spread fame. May his son Lada Khan, versed in the Kama Shastra, or Scripture of Love, and having his feet rubbed with the diadems of other kings, be ever victorious!

The great princely sage and arch-poet, Kalyana Malla versed in all the arts, after consulting many wise and holy men, and having examined the opinions of many poets, and extracted the essence of their wisdom, composed, with a view of pleasing his sovereign, a work

[2] The Sakit, or female principle, representing the aptitude of conception and continuation, becomes the wives of the gods in Hindu mythology. Thus in the Shavya-Purana, Shiva says, "from the supreme spirit proceed Parusha" (the generative or male principle), "and Parkriti" (the productive, or female principle), "and by them was produced the universe, the manifestation of the one god." For its origin we must go back to the Chaldaeo-Babylonian System.

which was called Ananga Ranga[3]. May it ever be appreciated by the discerning, for it hath been dedicated to those who are desirous of studying the art and mystery of man's highest enjoyment, and to those who are best acquainted with the science and practice of dalliance and love-delight.

It is true that no joy in the world of mortals can compare with that derived from the knowledge of the Creator. Second, however, and subordinate only to this, are the satisfaction and pleasure arising from the possession of a beautiful woman. Men, it is true, marry for the sake of undisturbed congress, as well as for love and comfort, and often they obtain handsome and attractive wives. But they do not give them plenary contentment, nor do they themselves thoroughly enjoy their charms. The reason of which is, that they are purely ignorant of the Scripture of Cupid, the Kama Shastra; and, despising the difference between the several kinds of women, they regard them only in an animal point of view. Such men must be looked upon as foolish and unintelligent; and this book is composed with the object of preventing lives and loves being wasted in similar manner, and the benefits to be derived from its study are set forth in the following verses:—

"The man who knoweth the Art of Love, and who understandeth the thorough and varied enjoyment of woman;

"As advancing age cooleth his passions, he learneth

---

[3] This title has been explained: see also Ward III. 179. Kama was the son of Maya (= Illusion, the attracting powers of Matter, Maia the mother of Mercury), he married Rati (Affection, vulgarised in our "rut") and is bosom-friend to Vasanta, Basant or Spring.

to think of his Creator, to study religious subjects, and to acquire divine knowledge:

"Hence he is freed from further transmigration of souls; and when the tale of his days is duly told, he goeth direct with his wife to the Svarga (heaven)."

And thus all you who read this book shall know how delicious an instrument is woman, when artfully played upon; how capable she is of producing the most exquisite harmony; of executing the most complicated variations and of giving the divinest pleasures.

Finally, let it be understood that every Shloka (stanza) of this work has a double signification, after the fashion of the Vedanta, and may be interpreted in two ways, either mystical or amatory.

THE

HINDU ART

OF LOVE

CHAPTER I

Of the Four Orders of Women.

FIRST, let it be understood, that women must be divided into four classes of temperament. These are:—

1. Padmini;
2. Chitrini;
3. Shankhini; and
4. Hastini.

The same correspond with the four different phases of Moksha, or Release from further Transmigration. The first is Sayujyata, or absorption into the essence of the Deity; the second is Samipyata, nearness to the Deity, the being born in the Divine Presence; the third is Sarupata, or resemblance to the Deity in limbs and material body; the fourth and last is Salokata, or residence in the heaven of some especial god.

For the name of woman is Nari, which, being interpreted, means "No A'ri", or foe; and such is Moksha, or absorption, because all love it and it loves all mankind.

Padmini, then, means Sayujyata, also called Khadgini-Moksha (Sword-release), the absorption of man into the Narayan (godhead), who lives in the Khshirabdi, or Milksea, one of the Seven Oceans, and from whose naval sprang the Padma, or Lotus-flower.

Chitrini is Samipyata-Moksha, like those who, having been incarnated as gods, perform manifold and wonderful works. Shankhini is Sarupata-Moksha, even as the man who takes the form of Vishnu, bears upon his body the Shankha (conch shell), the Chakra or discus, and other emblems of that god. The Hastini is Salokata-Moksha, for she is what residence in Vishnu's heaven is to those of the fourth class who have attributes and properties, shape and form, hands and feet.

Personal Peculiarities of the Four Classes.

And now learn ye by these words to distinguish from one another the four orders of woman-kind.

She in whom the following signs and symptoms appear, is called Padmini, or Lotus-woman.[1] Her face is pleasing as the full moon; her body, well clothed with flesh, is soft as the Shiras[2] or mustard-flower; her skin

---

[1] Evidently the nervous temperament, with due admixture of the bilious and sanguine.

[2] A lofty tree with soft and fragrant pollen.

is fine, tender and fair as the yellow lotus, never dark-coloured, though resembling, in the effervescence and purple light of her youth, the cloud about to burst. Her eyes are bright and beautiful as the orbs of the fawn, well-cut, and with reddish corners. Her bosom is hard, full and high; her neck is goodly shaped as the conch-shell, so delicate that the saliva can be seen through it; her nose is straight and lovely, and three folds of wrinkles cross her middle, about the umbilical region. Her Yoni[3] resembles the open lotus-bud, and her Love-seed (Kama-salila, the water of life)[4] is perfumed like the lily which has newly burst. She walks with swan-like gait, and her voice is low and musical as the note of the Kokila-bird[5]; she delights in white raiment, in fine jewels, and in rich dresses. She eats little, sleeps lightly and, being as respectable and religious as she is clever and courteous she is ever anxious to worship the gods, and to enjoy the conversation of Brahmans. Such, then, is the Padmini, or Lotus-woman.

The Chitrini, or Art-woman[6], is of the middle size, neither short nor tall, with bee-black hair, thin, round, shell-like neck; tender body; waist lean-girthed as the lion's; hard, full breasts; well-turned thighs and heavily made hips. The hair is thin about the Yoni, the Mons Veneris being soft, raised and round. The Kama-salila

[3] The Yoni the feminine opposite to the Linga (Priapus) or male apparatus.

[4] See note, chap. iv., on the Hindu ideas of human sperm, and for the vermicules of the Yoni, chap. iii., sec. 3.

[5] Usually known as the Indian cuckoo, though its voice is harsh and disagreeable; in poetry and romance it takes the place of the bulbul of Persia, and the nightingale of Europe.

[6] The sanguine temperament.

(love seed) is hot, and has the perfume of honey, producing from its abundance a sound during the venereal rite. Her eyes roll, and her walk is coquettish, like the swing of an elephant, whilst her voice is that of the peacock[7]. She is fond of pleasure and variety; she delights in singing and in every kind of accomplishment, especially the arts manual; her carnal desires, are not strong, and she loves her "pets", parrots, Mainas and other birds. Such is the Chitrini, or Art-woman.

The Shankhini[8], or Conch-woman, is of bilious temperament, her skin being always hot and tawny, or dark yellow-brown; her body is large, or waist thick, and her breasts small; her head, hands, and feet are thin and long, and she looks out of the corners of her eyes. Her Yoni is ever moist with Kama-salila, which is distinctly salt, and the cleft is covered with thick hair. Her voice is hoarse and harsh, of the bass or contralto type; her gait is precipitate; she eats with moderation and she delights in clothes, flowers and ornaments of red colour. She is subject to fits of amorous passion, which make her head hot and her brain confused[9], and at the moment of enjoyment, she thrusts her nails into her husband's flesh. She is of choleric constitution, hard-

[7] Meaning excellent as that of the Peacock, which is not disliked by the Hindus as by Europeans. They associate it with the breaking of the rainy monsoon, which brings joy to the thirsty earth and sun-parched men.

[8] The bilious temperament

[9] So Apollonius of Rhodes, describing the passion of Medeia, says: —"The fire which devours her, attacks all her nerves, and makes itself felt even behind the head in that spot where pain is most poignant when an extreme fervour seizes on all the senses."

hearted, insolent and vicious; irascible, rude and ever addicted to finding fault. Such is the Shankhini, or Conch-woman.

The Hastini is short of stature; she has a stout, coarse body, and her skin, if fair, is of a dead white; her hair is tawny, her lips are large; her voice is harsh, choked, and throaty (*voix de gorge*) and her neck is bent. Her gait is slow, and she walks in a slouching manner; often the toes of one foot are crooked. Her Kama-salila has the savour of the juice which flows in the spring from the elephant's temples. She is tardy in the Art of Love, and can be satisfied only by prolonged congress, in fact, the longer the better, but it will never suffice her. She is gluttonous, shameless, and irascible. Such is the Hastini, or elephant-woman.[10]

The days of greatest enjoyment for the Four Classes

Having thus laid down the four classes of woman-kind, Kalyana Malla, the arch-poet, proceeds to give a table of the time in which each order derives the greatest amount of pleasure from the venereal rite. These periods must be learnt by heart, and students will remember that on the other days not specified, no amount

[10] "Elephant"-woman, because the animal being called the "handed one," from the use of the trunk, and Hastini corresponds with Karami, from kara, a hand. She is "mulier nigris dignissima barris," and of the lymphatic or lowest temperament. These divisions represent, we have noted, roughly and unscientifically, the four European temperaments, nervous, sanguine, bilious and lymphatic. In a future chapter, the three Hindu temperaments will be discussed.

of congress will satisfy passions. Read, then, and master
the elements.

TABLE[11]

Pratipada 1st day	Dvitiya 2nd day	Chaturthi 4th day	Panchami 5th day	Satisfy the Padmini
Shasbati 6th day	Ashtami 8th day	Dashami 10th day	Dwadashi 12th day	Satisfy the Chatrini
Tritiya 3rd day	Saptami 7th day	Ekadashi 11th day	Trayodasi 13th day	Satisfy the Shankhini
Navami 9th day	Chaturdashi 14th day	Purnima Full Moon	Amavasya New Moon	Satisfy the Hastini

SECTION IV

Of the hours which give the highest enjoyment

Women, be it observed, differ greatly in the seasons
which they prefer for enjoyment, according to their
classes and temperaments. The Padmini, for instance,
takes no satisfaction in night congress; indeed, she is
thoroughly averse to it. Like the Surya Kamala (day-
lotus) which opens its eyes to the sunlight, so she is
satisfied even by a boy-husband in the bright hours.
The Chitrini and the Shankhini are like the Chandra
Kamala, or night-lotus, that expands to the rays of the
moon; and the Hastini, who is the coarsest, ignores all
these delicate distinctions.

[11] The days (Tithi) are those of the lunar fortnight: the Pratipada,
for instance, being the first, when the moon's increase and wane
begin.

18

The following tables, then, show the Pahar,[12] or watch of the night and day, during which the four classes of women derive the greatest pleasure.

TABLE I

Regulating the Night Hours

1st Pahar 6—9 p.m.	2nd Pahar 9—12 p.m.	3rd Pahar 12—3 a.m.	4th Pahar 3—6 a.m.
,,	,,	,,	The Padmini
The Chitrini	,,	,,	,,
,,	,,	The Shankhini	,,
The Hastini	The Hastini	The Hastini	The Hastini

TABLE II

Regulating the Day Hours

1st Pahar 6—9 a.m.	2nd Pahar 9—12 a.m.	3rd Pahar 12—3 p.m.	4th Pahar 3—6 p.m.
The Padmini	The Padmini	The Padmini	The Padmini
,,	,,	The Hastini	The Hastini

And here it will be observed that the Chitrini and the Shankhini derive no satisfaction from day congress.

[12] As amongst the classics, day and night are divided by the Hindus with eight watches, each of seven ghari, or hours (1 ghari = 24I).

Thus did the arch-poet, Kalyana Malla, relate unto Ladkhan Rajah how women are divided into four classes, each of which has its own peculiarity of body and mind, and its several times of enjoyments, according to the state of the moon and the hour of the day or night.

CHAPTER II

OF THE VARIOUS SEATS OF PASSION
IN WOMEN

AND, further, let men know that passion resides in different parts and members of the woman's person, and that by applying to these the necessary Chandrakala[1] or preparatory *attouchements*, great comfort and pleasure are experienced by both husband and wife. On the other hand, if the process placed in the table opposite the respective days of the lunar fortnight be not performed, neither sex will be thoroughly satisfied; indeed, both will be disposed to lust after strange embraces, and thus they will be led by adultery into quarrels, murders, and other deadly sins, all of which may be avoided by studying and bearing in mind the Chandrakala.

Passion resides in the woman's right side during the

[1] Chandrakala is properly a digit, or one-sixteenth of the lunar orb.

General Table III

Shuklapaksha or light fortnight; right side		The touches by which passion is satisfied	Krishnapaksha or dark fortnight; left side	
Day	Place		Place	Day
15th	Head and hair	Hold hair, and caress the head and finger-tips	Head and hair	1st
14th	Right eye	Kiss and fondle	Left eye	2nd
13th	Lower lip	Kiss, bite and chew softly	Upper lip	3rd
12th	Right cheek	Do.	Left cheek	4th
11th	Throat	Scratch gently with nails	Throat	5th
10th	Side	Do.	Side	6th
9th	Breasts	Hold in hands and gently knead	Breasts	7th
8th	All bosom	Tap softly with base of fist	All bosom	8th
7th	Navel	Pat softly with open palm	Navel	9th
6th	Nates	Hold, squeeze and tap with fist	Nates	10th
5th	Yoni	Work with friction of Linga	Yoni	11th
4th	Knee	Press with application of knee and fillip with finger	Knee	12th
3rd	Calf of leg	Press with application of calf and fillip with finger	Calf and leg	13th
2nd	Foot	Press with toe, and thrust the latter	Foot	14th
1st	Big toe	Do.	Big toe	15th

Shuklapaksha, the first or light fortnight of the lunar month, from new moon to full, including the fifteenth day. The reverse is the case on the dark fortnight, including its first day, and lasting from the full to the new moon. The shifting is supposed to take place by the action of light and darkness, otherwise the site of passion would be one and the same.

Now from generals, Kalyana Malla, the poet, proceeds to particulars, and supplies details concerning the four different classes of women. He begins with the Padmini, and shows, firstly, in what limb or member passion resides; and, secondly, by what process it can be satisfied. The husband must continue his action till he sees the body-hair bristle, and hears the Sitkara[2]—the inarticulate sound produced by drawing in the air between the closed teeth. Thus he will know that the paroxysm has taken place, and the beloved one is thoroughly satisfied.

[2] Called Sitkara from the sound "S't! s't! s't! s't!" as a person breathing hard or drawing in cold air between the teeth, thus making an inarticulate sound. Full particulars concerning it will be found in Chapter IX.

TABLE IV

Showing the Manipulations of the Padmini

Member	Pratipada 1st day	Dvitiya 2nd day	Chaturthi 4th day	Panchami 5th day
Throat	Hug with force	,,	,,	,,
Cheek	Kiss and scratch	Kiss and scratch	,,	,,
Hair	,,	,,	,,	Stroke slowly with right hand
Waist	Apply nails and scratch	,,	,,	,,
Breast	,,	,,	Scratch gently	,,
Back	Scratch & tap with fist	,,	,,	,,
Bosom	,,	Press with nails	Squeeze and knead	Press and rub
Side	Scratch and press with nails	,,	,,	,,
Thigh	,,	Scratch and press with nails	,,	,,
Belly	Scratch and press with nails	,,	,,	,,
Arm	,,	,,	Jerk suddenly and twitch	,,
Lip	Bite softly and kiss	Kiss	Bite softly and suck	Bite softly
Nipple	,,	,,	,,	Kiss, pinch softly and rub with thumb and fore-finger
Space between eyes	Kiss	,,	,,	,,
Foot	,,	Scratch and press with nails	,,	,,

24

TABLE V

Showing the Manipulations of the Chitrini

Member	Shasti 6th day	Ashtami 8th day	Dashami 15th day	Dwadashi 12th day
Yoni	,,	Insert Linga	Rub and scratch with left hand	,,
Lower lip	Kiss	,,	,,	Bite very gently
Throat	Embrace	Clasp firmly with hands	Scratch and pass fingers over it	Embrace firmly
Waist	Scratch and press with nails	,,	Pass left hand over it and rub	,,
Navel	,,	Pinch with nails and fingers	,,	,,
Lip	,,	Bite quickly and repeatedly	,,	,,
Breast		Hold in hand	Pass left hand over it and rub	,,
Ear	,,	,,	Caress with left hand	Set nails upon it
Thigh	,,	,,	Rub with left hand	,,
Middle of body	,,	,,	Pass left hand over it and rub	,,
Back	,,	,,	Rub with left hand and tap with fist	,,
Nates	,,	,,	,,	,,
Forehead	,,	,,	Kiss strongly	,,
Chest	,,	,,	,,	Kiss and pat
Eye				Do something that will make the eyes close rapidly
Hair	,,	,,	,,	Pull gently

TABLE VI

Showing the Manipulations of the Shankhini

Member	Tritiya 3rd day	Saptami 7th day	Ekadashi 11th day	Trayodashi 13th day
Body generally	Twist it about	Embrace firmly	Clasp with force	,,
Lower lip	Bite	,,	,,	,,
Arm	?	,,	,,	,,
Breasts	Scratch roughly till marks are left	,,	,,	Squeeze till she makes the sound of Sitkara
Belly	,,	Scratch and press with nails	,,	,,
Chest	,,	Press with nails and caress	,,	,,·
Throat	,,	Scratch and press with nails	,,	,,
Ear	,,	Press with nails	,,	,,
Foot	,,	Press so as to leave nail-marks	,,	,,
Mouth or face	,,	Kiss	,,	,,
Yoni	,,	Apply Linga with force	Apply Linga as it were with a blow[3]	,,
Lip	,,	,,	Kiss and suck	,,
Inch below head	,,	,,	,,	Write upon it, as it were, with nails
Lower edge of Yoni	,,	,,	,,	,,

[3] In the original Sanskrit and in all the translations there is an illusion to the practice described by Juvenal (IX. 4).

Ravola dum Rhodopes uda terit inguina barba.

TABLE VII

Showing the Manipulations of the Hastini

Member	Navami 9th day	Chaturdashi 14th day	Purnima Full Moon	Amavasya New Moon
Yoni	Thrust violently with Linga or evenrubhard with hand	Scratch, press in member till her waist bends	,,	Manipulate and pull open like a flower
Navel	Rub and frequently pass hand over	,,	,,	,,
Lip	Kiss and suck	,,	Kiss in various ways[4]	Kiss in various ways
Side	Press with fingers & scratch very softly	,,	,,	,,
Breast	Rub, squeeze twist, & make it very small	,,	Pull hard	Scratch till it bears nail-marks
Chest	,,	,,	Scratch and leave marks	Scratch and leave marks
Nipple	,,	,,	Kiss and rub with thumb and forefinger	Pass hand over it and rub with thumb and forefinger
Body generally	,,	,,	Embrace in various ways	Embrace in various ways and press
Eye	,,	Kiss	Kiss	Kiss
Armpit	,,	,,	Scratch and tickle	Scratch and tickle

Here end the tables of the Chandrakala, by the proper study of which men may satisfy women, and thereby subject the most strong-minded to their will.

4 Alluding to what Shakespeare calls "kissing with th'inner lip."

CHAPTER III

OF THE DIFFERENT KINDS OF
MEN AND WOMEN

SECTION I
Men

THERE are three kinds of men, namely, the Shastra, or the Hare-man; the Vrishabha, or Bull-man, and the Ashwa, or Horse-man.[1] These may be described by explanation of their nature, and by enumeration of their accidents.

The Shasha is known by a Linga which in erection does not exceed six finger-breaths, or about three inches. His figure is short and spare, but well-proportioned in shape and make; he has small hands, knees, feet, loins and thighs, the latter being darker than the rest of the skin. His features are clear and well proportioned; his

---

[1] These divisions again appear to represent the nervous, bilious and sanguine temperament. Some MSS. divide men only by the three Linga-lengths of 6, 9 and 12 finger breadths; the latter (12 widths) would be of African or Negro dimensions.

face is round, his teeth are short and fine, his hair is silky, and his eyes are large and well-opened. He is of a quiet disposition; he does good for virtue's sake; he looks forward to making a name; he is humble in demeanour; his appetite for food is small, and he is moderate in carnal desires. Finally, there is nothing offensive in his Kama-salila or semen.

The Vrishabha is known by a Linga of nine fingers in length, or four inches and a half. His body is robust and tough, like that of a tortise; his chest is fleshy, his belly is hard, and the frogs of the upper arms are turned so as to be brought in front. His forehead is high, his eyes large and long, with pink corners, and the palms of his hands are red. His disposition is cruel and violent, restless and irascible, and his Kama-salila is every ready.

The Ashwa is known by a Linga of twelve fingers, or about six inches long. He is tall and large-framed, but not fleshy, and his delight is in big and robust women, never in those of delicate form. His body is hard as iron, his chest is broad, full, and muscular; his body below the hips is long, and the same is the case with his mouth and teeth, his neck and ears; whilst his hands and fingers are remarkably so. His knees are somewhat crooked, and this distortion may also be observed in the nails of his toes. His hair is long, coarse and thick. His look is fixed and hard, without changing form, and his voice is deep like that of a bull. He is reckless in spirit, passionate and covetous, gluttonous, volatile, lazy, and full of sleep. He walks slowly, placing one foot in front of the other. He cares little for the venereal rite, except when the spasm approaches. His Kama-salila is copious, salt, and goat-like.

Women

And as men are divided into three classes by the length of the Linga, so the four orders of women, Padmini, Chitrini, Shankhini and Hastini, may be subdivided into three kinds, according to the depth and extent of the Yoni. These are the Mrigi, also called Harini, the Deer-woman; the Vadava or Ashvini, Mare-woman; and the Karini, or Elephant-woman.

The Mrigi has a Yoni six fingers deep. Her body is delicate, with girlish aspect, soft and tender. Her head is small and well-proportioned; her bosom stands up well; her stomach is thin and drawn in; her thighs and Mons Veneris are fleshy, and her build below the hips is solid, whilst her arms from the shoulder downwards are large and rounded. Her hair is thick and curly; her eyes are black as the dark lotus-flower; her nostrils are fine; her cheeks and ears are large; her hands, feet, and lower lip are ruddy, and her fingers are straight. Her voice is that of the Kokila bird, and her gait the rolling of the elephant. She eats moderately, but is much addicted to the pleasure of love; she is affectionate but jealous, and she is active in mind when not subdued by her passions. Her Kama-salila has the pleasant perfume of the lotus-flower.

The Vadava or Ashvini numbers nine fingers depth. Her body is delicate; her arms are thick from the shoulders downwards; her breasts and hips are broad and fleshy, and her umbilical region is high-raised, but without protuberant stomach. Her hands and feet are red like flowers, and well-proportioned. Her head slopes forwards and is covered with long and straight hair; her forehead is retreating; her neck is long and much bent; her throat, eyes, and mouth are broad, and her eyes are like the petals of the dark lotus. She has a graceful walk, and she loves sleep and good living. Though choleric and versatile, she is affectionate to her husband; she does not easily arrive at the venereal spasm, and her Kama-salila is perfumed like the lotus.

The Karini has a Yoni twelve fingers in depth. Unclean in her person, she has large breasts; her nose, ears, and throat are long and thick; her cheeks are blown or expanded; her lips are long and bent outwards (*bordes*); her eyes are fierce and yellow-tinged; her face is broad; her hair is thick and somewhat blackish; her feet, hands, and arms are short and fat; and her teeth are large and sharp as a dog's. She is noisy when eating; her voice is hard and harsh; she is gluttonous in the extreme, and her joints crack with every movement. Of a wicked and utterly shameless disposition, she never hesitates to commit sin. Excited and disquieted by carnal desires, she is not easily satisfied, and requires congress unusually protracted. Her Kama-salila is very abundant, and it suggests the juice which flows from the elephant's temples.

The wise man will bear in mind that all these characteristics are not equally well defined and their proportions can be known only by experience. Mostly the temperaments are mixed; often we find a combination of two and in some cases even of three. Great study, therefore, is required in judging by the absence or presence of the signs and symptoms, to choose the Chandrakala and other manipulations proper to the several differences, as without such judgment the consequences of congress are not satisfactory. Thus the student is warned that the several distinctions of Padmani, Chitrini, Shankhini and Hastini; of Shasta, Vrishabha, and Ashva, and of Mrigi (Harini), Vadava (Ashvini), and Karini are seldom found pure, and that it is his duty to learn the proportions in which they combine.

Before proceeding to the various acts of congress, the symptoms of the orgasm in women must be laid down. As soon as she commences to enjoy pleasure, the eyes are half closed and watery; the body waxes cold; the breath after being hard and jerky, is expired in sobs or sighs; the lower limbs are limply stretched out after a period of rigidity; a rising and outflow of love and affection appear, with kisses and sportive gestures; and, finally, she seems as if about to swoon. At such time, a distaste for further embraces and blandishments becomes manifest; then the wise know that, the paroxysm having taken place, the woman has enjoyed plenary satisfaction; consequently, they refrain from further congress.

SECTION III

Of Congress

Men and women, being, according to the above measurements, of three several divisions, it results that there are nine conditions under which congress takes place. Of these, however, four, being unusual, may be neglected, and attention is required only for the five following:

1. Samana is when the proportions of both lovers are alike and equal; hence there is plenary satisfaction to both.

2. Uchha is that excess of proportion in the man which renders congress hard and difficult and therefore does not content the woman.

3. Nichha, meaning literally *hollow* or *low*, and metaphorically when the man is deficient in size, gives but little contentment to either lover.

4. Anti-uchha is an exaggeration of Uchha; and

5. Anti-nichha is an exaggeration of Nichha.

The following table divides the congress of the several dimensions into three categories; which are respectively entitled Uttama, the best; Madhyama, the middling; and Kanishtha, the worst.

From an inspection of these tables, it is abundantly evident that the greatest happiness consist in the correspondence of dimensions, and that the discomfort increases with the ratio of difference. And of this fact the reason is palpable.

Table VIII

Applicable to the Shasha, or Hare-man

Dimensional Names	Actual dimensions of members	Category
Shasha Mrigi }	6 fingers long 6 fingers deep	Uttama
Shasha Vadva or Ashvini }	6 fingers long 9 fingers deep	Madhyama
Shasha Karini }	6 fingers long 12 fingers deep	Kanishtha

TABLE IX

Applicable to the Vrishabha, or Bull-man

Dimensional Names	Actual dimensions of members	Category
Vrishabha Ashvini }	9 fingers long 9 fingers deep	Uttama
Vrishabha Harini }	9 fingers long 6 fingers deep	Madhyama
Vrishabha Karini }	9 fingers long 12 fingers deep	Kanishtha

TABLE X

Applicable to the Ashwa, or Horse-man

Dimensional Names	Actual dimensions of members	Category
Ashva Karini }	12 fingers long 12 fingers deep	Uttama
Ashva Ashvini }	12 fingers long 9 fingers deep	Madhyama
Ashva Harini }	12 fingers long 6 fingers deep	Kanishtha

There are three species of vermicules bred by blood in the Yoni[2] and these are either Sukshma (small) Madhyama (middling), or Adhikabala (large). In their several proportions they produce a prurience and titillation, wherefrom springs that carnal desire which is caused to cease only by congress. And thus it is that a Linga of small dimensions fails to satisfy. On the other hand, excess of length offends the delicacy of the parts,

[2] A fair anticipation of the spermatozoa: see terminal note of Chap. iv.

and produces pain rather than pleasure. But the proportion of enjoyment arises from the exact adaptation of the Linga, especially when the diameter agrees with the extension, and when the vigour of tension enables the husband to turn his mind towards the usual arts which bring women under subjection.

Of other Minor Distinctions in Congress

Each of the foregoing nine forms of congress is subdivided into nine other classes, which will now be noticed.

There are three forms of Vissrishti, or the emission of Kama-salila, both in men and women, viewed with respect to length or shortness of time:

1. Chirasambhava-vissrishti is that which occupies a great length of time.

2. Madhyasambhava-vissrishti is that which is accomplished within a moderate period.

3. Shighrasambhava-vissrishti is that which takes a short time to finish.

Again, there are three degrees of Vega, that is to say, force of carnal desire, resulting from mental or vital energy and acting upon men and women. In order to make this clear, a comparison may be instituted. Hunger, for instance, is felt by all human beings, but it affects them differently. Some must satisfy it at once, without which they are ready to lose their senses; others can endure it for a moderate extent, whilst others suffer from it but little. The Vegas, or capacities of enjoyment, are:

1. Chanda-vega, furious appetite or impulse; the highest capacity.

2. Madhyama-vega, or moderate desires.

3. Manda-vega, slow or cold concupiscence; the lowest capacity.

The woman who possesses Chanda-vega, may be known by her ever seeking carnal enjoyment; she must enjoy it frequently and she will not be satisfied with a single orgasm. If deprived of it, she will appear like one out of her senses. The reverse is she who has Manda-vega, and who seems to find in it so little enjoyment that she always denies herself to her husband. And the owner of Madhyama-vega is the most fortunate, as she is free from either excess.

Again, there are three Kriyas, acts or processes which bring on the orgasm in men and women; these are:

1. Chirodaya-kriya, is applied to the efforts which continue long before they bear any result.

2. Madhyodaya-kriya, those which act in a moderate time.

3. Laghudaya-kriya, the shortest.

Thus we may observe there are nine several forms of congress, according to the length and depth of the organs. There are also nine, determined by the longer or shorter period required to induce the orgasm and there are nine which arise from the Kriyas or processes which lead to the conclusion. Altogether we have twenty-seven kinds of congress, which, by multiplying the nine species and the three periods, give a grand total of two hundred and forty-three ($9 \times 9 = 81 \times 3 = 243$).

CHAPTER IV

DESCRIPTION OF THE GENERAL QUALITIES, CHARACTERISTICS, TEMPERAMENTS, ETC., OF WOMEN

THE following table will show the peculiarities of women according to the four periods of life during which she is open to love. It may be premised that she is called Kanya from birth to the age of eight years, which is the time of Balyavastha, or childhood;

TABLE XI

Showing Qualities attached to the several Ages

Age	Name	Regarding art of love	Kind of Congress preferred	How subjected
11—16 years	Bala	Fit	In darkness	By flowers, small presents, gifts of betel, and so forth
16—30 years	Taruni	Do.	In light	By gifts of dresses, pearls and ornaments
30—55 years	Praudha	Fit	Both in darkness and light	By attention, politeness, kindness and love
Beyond 55 years	Viddha	Unfit	Becomes sick and infirm	By flattery

and Gauri, after the white goddess Parvati, from that period to her eleventh year; Tarunyavastha when she becomes marriageable: then follow Yavavastha, young-womanhood, and Vreuddhavastha, old-womanhood.

And further observe that there are three temperaments of women, as shown by the following characteristics:

The signs of Kapha (lymphatic or phlegmatic diathesis) are bright eyes, teeth and nails; the body is well preserved, and the limbs do not lose their youthful form. The Yoni is cool and hard, fleshy, yet delicate; and there is love and regard for the husband. Such is the lymphatic, or the highest temperament.[1]

The next is the Pitta, or bilious diathesis. The woman whose bosom and nates are flaccid and pendant, not orbiculate; whose skin is white, whilst her eyes and nails are red; whose perspiration is sour, and whose Yoni is hot and relaxed; who is well versed in the arts of congress, but who cannot endure it for a long time, and whose temper is alternately and suddenly angry and joyous, such a one is held to be of the Pitta or bilious temperament.

She whose body is dark, hard, and coarse; whose eyes and finger nails are blackish, and whose Yoni, instead of being smooth, is rough as the tongue of a cow; she whose laugh is harsh; whose mind is set on gluttony; who is volatile and loquacious, whilst in congress she can hardly be satisfied, that woman is of the Vata or windy temperament, the worst of all.

Furthermore, women require to be considered in connection with the previous state of their existence; the

[1] In old European physiology it ranked lowest.

Satva, or disposition inherited from a former life, and which influences their worldly natures.

The Devasatva-stri, who belongs to the Gods, is cheerful and lively, pure-bodied and clean, with perspiration perfumed like the lotus-flower; she is clever, wealthy and industrious, of sweet speech and benevolent, always delighting in good works; her mind is sound as her body, nor is she ever tired or displeased by her friends.

The Gandharvasarva-stri, who derives a name from the Gandharvas, or heavenly minstrels, is beautiful of shape, patient in mind, delighting in purity; wholly given to perfumes, fragrant substances and flowers, to singing and playing, to rich dress and fair ornaments, to sport and amorous play, especially to the Vilasa, one of the classes of feminine actions which indicate the passion of love.

The Yakshasatva-stri, who derives a name from the demi-god presiding over the gardens and treasures of Kuvera[2] has large and fleshy breasts, with a skin fair as the white champa-flower (*michelia champac*); she is fond of flesh and liquor; devoid of shame and decency; passionate and irascible, and at all hours greedy for congress.

The Munushyasatva-stri, who belongs essentially to humanity, delights in the pleasures of friendship and hospitality. She is respectable and honest, her mind is free from guile, and she is never wearied of religious actions, vows, and penances.

The Pisachasatva-stri, who is concerned with that class of demons, has a short body, very dark and hot, with a forehead ever wrinkled; she is unclean in her person,

[2] The Hindu Plutus, god of wealth.

greedy, fond of flesh and forbidden things, and, however much enjoyed, she is ever eager of congress, like a harlot.

The Nagasatva-stri, or snake-woman, is always in hurry and confusion; her eyes look drowsy; she yawns over and over again, and she sighs with deep-drawn respiration; her mind is forgetful and she lives in doubt and suspicion.

The Kakasatva-stri, who retains the characteristics of the crow, ever rolls her eyes about as if in pain; throughout the day she wants food; she is silly, unhappy and unreasonable, spoiling everything that she touches.

The Vanarasatva-stri, or monkey-woman, rubs her eyes throughout the day, grinds and chatters with her teeth, and is very lively, active, and mercurial.

The Kharasatva-stri, who preserves the characteristics of the ass,[3] is unclean in her person, and avoids bathing, washing, and pure raiment: she cannot give a direct answer, and she speaks awkwardly and without reason, because her mind is crooked. Therefore she pleases no one.

The subject of the Satvas is one requiring careful study, for the characteristics are ever varying, and only experience can determine the class to which women belonged

[3] The Semitic races domesticated the ass, and recognised its admirable qualities; they treated it with due respect, and they were not ashamed of being compared with it—*e.g.*, "Issachar is a strong ass." The early Egyptian kings (B.C. 4000–1000) had no horses in their invading hosts, and the law of Moses seems to condemn the use. The "Equus Caballus" was conquered and utilized by the Caucasians in Central Asia, and they overwhelmed its rival with abuse and contempt, attributing its creation to Vishvakarma, who caricatured the work of the gods.

in the former life, and which has coloured their bodies and minds in this state of existence.

The woman whose bosom is hard and fleshy, who appears short from the fullness of her frame, and looks bright and light-coloured, such a one is known to enjoy daily congress with her husband.

The woman who, being thin, appears very tall and somewhat dark, whose limbs and body are unenergetic and languid, the effect of involuntary chastity, such a one is "Virahini," who suffers from long separation from her husband and from the want of conjugal embraces.

A woman who eats twice as much as a man, is four times more reckless and wicked, six times more resolute and obstinate, and eight times more violent in carnal desire. She can hardly control her lust of congress, despite the shame which is natural to the sex.

The following are the signs by which the wise know that a woman is amorous: She rubs and repeatedly smoothes her hair (so that it may look well). She scratches her head (that notice may be drawn to it). She strokes her own cheeks (so as to entice her husband). She draws her dress over her bosom, apparently to re-adjust it, but leaves her breasts partly exposed. She bites her lower lip, chewing it, as it were. At times she looks ashamed without a cause (the result of her own warm fancies), and she sits quietly in the corner (engrossed, by concupiscence). She embraces her female friends, laughing loudly and speaking sweet words, with jokes and jests, to which she desires a return in kind. She kisses and hugs young children, especially boys. She smiles with one cheek, loiters in her gait, and unnecessarily stretches herself under some pretence or other. At times she looks at her shoulders and under her arms. She stammers, and does not speak clearly and distinctly. She sighs and sobs without reason and she yawns whenever she wants tobacco, food, or sleep. She even throws herself in her husband's way and will not readily get out of his path.

The following are the eight signs of indifference to be noted in womankind: When worldly passion begins to subside, the wife does not look straight between her husband's eyes. If anything be asked of her, she shows unwillingness to reply. If the man draw near her, and look happy, she feels pained. If he departs from her she shows symptoms of satisfaction. When seated upon the bedstead, she avoids amatory blandishments and lies down quietly to sleep. When kissed or toyed with she jerks away her face or her form. She cherishes malicious feelings towards her husband's friends; and finally, she has no respect nor reverence for his family. When these signs are seen, let it be known that the wife is already weaned from conjugal desires.

The following are the principal causes which drive women to deviate from the right way, and to fall into the society of profligates: 1. Remaining, when grown up, in her Maher, or mother's house, as opposed to that of her husband's parents. 2. Evil communication with the depraved of her own sex. 3. The prolonged absence of her husband. 4. Living in the society of vile and licentious men. 5. Poverty and the want of good food and dress. 6. Mental trouble, affliction, and unhappiness, causing her to become discontented and reckless.

The following are the fifteen principal causes which

make women unhappy: 1. The parsimony of parents and husbands, because the young are naturally generous. 2. Receiving too much respect or reverence when they are lighthearted; also being kept in awe by those with whom they would be familiar, and a too strict restraint as regards orderly and guarded deportment. 3. Trouble of disease and sickness. 4. Separation from the husband and the want of natural enjoyment. 5. Being made to work too hard. 6. Violence, inhumanity, and cruelty, such as beating. 7. Rough language and abuse. 8. Suspicion that they are inclined to evil. 9. Intimidation and threats of punishment for going astray. 10. Calumny, accusing of ill deeds, and using evil words about them. 11. Want of cleanliness in person or dress. 12. Poverty. 13. Grief and sorrow. 14. Impotence of the husband. 15. Disregard of time and place in the act of love.

The following are the twelve periods when women have the greatest desire for congress, and at the same time are most easily satisfied: 1. When tired by walking and exhausted with bodily exercise. 2. After a long want of intercourse with the husband, such as in the case of the Virahini. 3. When a month after childbirth has elapsed. 4. During the earlier stages of pregnancy. 5. When dull, idle and sleepy. 6. If recently cured of fever. 7. When showing signs of wantonness or bashfulness. 8. When feeling unusually merry and happy. 9. The Ritusnata, immediately before and after the monthly ailment.[4] 10. Maidens enjoyed for the first time. 11. Throughout the spring season. 12. During thunder, lightning and rain. At such times women are easily subjected to men.

[4] Ritu-snata is the woman, who, on the fourth day, has bathed and become pure.

And furthermore, learn that there are four kinds of the Priti, or love-tie connecting men and women:

1. Naisargiki-priti is that natural affection by which husband and wife cleave to each other like the links of an iron chain. It is a friendship amongst the good of both sexes.

2. Vishaya-priti is the fondness born in the woman, and increased by means of gifts, such as sweetmeats and delicacies, flowers, perfumery, and preparations of sandalwood, musk, saffron, and so forth. It partakes, therefore, of gluttony, sensuality and luxury.

3. Sama-priti is also so far sensual, as it arises from the equally urgent desires of both husband and wife.

4. Abhyasiki-priti is the habitual love bred by mutual society: it is shown by walking in fields, gardens and similar places; by attending together at worship, penances and self-imposed religious observances; and by frequenting sportive assemblies, plays and dances, where music and similar arts are practised.

And, moreover, let it be noted, that the desires of the woman being colder,[5] and slower to rouse than those of the man, she is not easily satisfied by a single act of congress; her slower powers of excitement demand prolonged embraces, and if these be denied her, she feels aggrieved. At the second act, however, her passions being thoroughly aroused, she finds the orgasm more violent, and then she is thoroughly contented. This state of things is clean reversed in the case of the man, who approaches

[5] This is the Hindu view: The Moslems hold that the desires of a woman are ten times stronger than those of a man. Both are right in certain exceptions; for instance the male is the stronger in dry climates, the female in the hot, damp and depressing.

the first act burning with love heat, which cools during the second, and which leaves him languid and disinclined for a third. But the wise do not argue therefrom, that the desires of the woman, as long as she is young and strong, are not at the full as real and urgent as those of the man. The custom of society and the shame of the sex may compel her to conceal them and even to boast that they do not exist; yet the man who has studied the Art of Love is never deceived by this cunning.

And here it is necessary to offer some description of the Yoni; it being of four kinds.

1. That which is soft inside as the filaments (pollen?) of the lotus-flower; this is the best.

2. That whose surface is studded with tender flesh-knots and similar rises.

3. That which abounds in rolls, wrinkles, and corrugations; and

4. That which is rough as the cow's tongue; this is the worst.

Moreover, in the Yoni there is an artery called Saspanda; which corresponds with that of the Linga, and which, when excited by the presence and energetic action of the latter, causes Kama-salila to flow. It is inside and towards the navel, and it is attached to certain roughnesses (thorns), which are peculiarly liable to induce the paroxysm when subjected to friction. The Madana-chatra (the clitoris)[6], in the upper part of the Yoni, is that

---

[6] The "Fons et scaturigo Veneris" of the classics. It need hardly be remarked that the Hindus, like the ancients in Europe, believed the Kama-salila of women to be in every way like that of men; the microscope was required for the detection of the spermatozoa in one sex only. "Clitoris" means "shutter"; and hence the French *clitoriser*, to tickle it.

portion which projects like the plantain-shoot sprouting from the ground; it is connected with the Mada-vahi (sperm-flowing) artery, and causes the latter to overflow. Finally, there is an artery, termed Purna-chandra, which is full of the Kama-salila, and to this the learned men of old attribute the monthly ailment.

CHAPTER V

CHARACTERISTICS OF THE WOMEN
OF VARIOUS LANDS

FURTHERMORE, after dividing women into many different classes, it will be desirable to consider them with reference to the countries in which they dwell. The remarks will be confined to the Arya-vartta, the Land of Men, bounded by the Himalaya (snowhouse) and Vindhya Mountains, the Kuru-Kshetra and Allahabad. And first of the woman of the Madhya-desha, the country between the Konkan and the Desha proper, whose chief cities are Puna (Poona), Nasik and Kolhapur.

The woman of the Middle Region has red nails, but her body is still redder. She dresses well and in various sorts of apparel. She is an excellent housekeeper, perfectly broken to manual labour and other works, and much given to religious ceremonies. Though wonderfully fond of, and skilful in, amatory dalliance, she is averse to the tricks of teeth and nails (biting and scratching).

The Maru (Malwa) woman likes to be enjoyed every day, and is well fitted for those who prefer the act of congress when long protracted. She is satisfied only by enduring embraces, which she greatly covets and desires, and the paroxysm must sometimes be induced by the touch of the fingers.

The woman of Mathra, Krishna's country, also called Abhira-deshra, the Cow-herds' Land, is fascinated by various forms of kissing. She delights in the closest embraces, and even in attouchments; but she has no tricks of tooth and nail.

The woman of Lata-desha (Lar or Larice of the Classics), the northern part of the Dakhan (Deccan), is delicate and handsome. She will dance with joy at the prospect of congress, and during the act, her movements of pleasure are frequent and violent. She is prompt in her embraces, and the venereal orgasm may readily be induced by gentle insertion, by striking with the hand, and by softly biting her lips.

The woman of Andhra-desha (Telangana) is so fascinating that she charms the stranger at first sight, and she is sweet in voice as she is beautiful of body. She delights in jests and dalliance, yet she is an utter stranger to shame, and she is one of the most wicked of her sex.

The woman of Koshalarashtra-desha (Audh or Oude) is very clever in the art of congress. She suffers much from prurience and titillation of the Yoni, and she desires lengthened embraces, which satisfy her only when the Linga is of unusual vigour.

The woman of Maharashtra (the Maratha country) and Patalaputa-desha is fond of giving amorous side-glances, of dress and ornaments, of junketting and garden trips. Ever smiling gently, airy and gay, full of jest and sport and amorous dalliance, she is yet somewhat destitute of shame. Affectionate and coquettish, she is a proficient in the toying of love.

The woman of Vanga (Bengal) and Gaura has a body soft and delicate as a flower; she is coquettish and volatile; she delights in kissing and embracing, at the same time that she hates being roughly or cruelly handled, and she has little desire for congress.

The woman of Utkala-desha (Orissa) is so beautiful that man is attracted to her at first sight, and her voice is soft as her body is delicate. She is loose and licentious, caring very little for decency in her devotion to love, at which time she becomes violent, disquieted and excessively inflamed; she delights in different postures to vary enjoyment, especially in the contrary form, that is when the lover is under the beloved, and she is easily satisfied, even by passing the fingers over her breasts.

The woman of Kamarupa-desha (Western Assam) has a soft body and sweet voice; her affections are warm, and she is well skilled in all the arts of love. During congress she abounds in the Kama-salila.

The Vana-stri, or forest woman (of the Bhills and other hill tribes), have stout bodies and healthy constitutions. They delight, whilst concealing their own defects and blemishes, their faults and follies, in exposing those of others.

The woman of Gurjara-desha (Gujrat, or Guzerat) is wise and sensible. She has beautiful features, and eyes proportioned as they ought to be; she delights in handsome dresses and ornaments, and though warm and devoted to the pleasures of love, she is easily satisfied by short congress.

The woman of Sindhu-desha (Sind), of Avanti-desha (Panjab or Aujein), and of Balhika-desha (Bahawalpur), has lively eyes, casting sidelong and amorous glances. She is volatile, irascible, and wicked, and the fierceness, violence, and heat of her desires are very hard to be satisfied.

The woman of Tirotpatna (or Tira-desha, Tirhoot in Central India) has eyes blooming like the flowers of the lake; she loves her husband fondly and her passion is inflamed by a single look; she is especially skilful in congress; she enjoys various ways and postures; and, by reason of her delicacy, she cannot endure rough or protracted embraces.

The woman of Pushpapura, of Madda-desha (the north-western part of Hindostan Proper), and of Tailanga-desha (Southern India), though a proficient in the art of love, is modest, and enjoys only her husband. Her form of passion is the Chanda-vega, and her amorousness is excessive; she communicates delight by "Nakhara," scratching, biting, and other signs of hot desire.

The woman of Dravia-desha (the Coromandel country, from Madras to Cape Comorin), of Sauvira, and of Malaya-desha (Malayalim) is well-proportioned in body and limbs, soft and delicate in make, and sweet of voice; she delights in clean raiment and fine dresses, and she is satisfied with short congress, although fearless, shameless, and headlong in wickedness.

The woman of Kamboj (Camboge) and Paundra-desha is tall, robust, and gross in body, and of wicked disposition; she is ignorant of the acts of congress accompanied by tricks of nail and tooth, and she is satisfied only by the violent application of a solid Linga.

The women of the Mlenchchhas (mixed races, or those not speaking Sanskrit like the Hindus), of Parvata, of Gandhara and of Kashmir (Cashmere), are distinguished by evil savour of body. They are wholly ignorant of toying and dalliance, of kissing and embracing; they care little for congress, and they are easily satisfied by short embraces.

It is only by study and experience of these women in different countries that the wise man learns to classify them according to their several characteristics to discern the Chandrakalas, or preparatory attouchments, which best suit races as well as individuals, and thus to endear himself to womankind.

CHAPTER VI

TREATING OF VASHIKARANA

VASHIKARANA is the art by which man or woman is rendered submissive and obedient to the fascinator, who for that purpose uses certain drugs and charms. And first the magic "Talaka."[1]

First Prescription

The holy sage Vatsyayana Muni[2] hath declared that whosoever will take the powder of sensitive plant, the

[1] This is a round sectarian mark, about the size of a wafer, which the Hindu applies to his forehead, after certain rites and prayers. The reader will find this chapter interesting on account of the various abominations which it contains. The underlying idea appears to be that if any secretion of the body, the fouler the better, can be secretly administered to a person of either sex, the result is the subjection of the patient to the adhibitor. The European reader will hardly believe how extensively this practice is carried out all over the East. No Persian will drink sherbet in the house of his future mother-in-law; and Jewish women, who are especially addicted to these practices, will mix their monthly blood in the philters which they give to men.

[2] The reader can now consult the Kama Sutra of the Sage Vatsyayana, translated from the Sanskrit in seven Parts, gr. in 8vo, with Preface, Introduction and concluding remarks, *Benares, printed for the Hindoo Kama Shastra Society,* 1883.

root of green lotus-flowers, the Bassia latifolia, and bar-
ley-flower; and, after mixing it up with some of his own
Kama-salila, will apply it as a sectarian mark to his forehead, such an one will subdue the world of women, and
she who looks upon his brow cannot fail to feel for him
the most eager desire.

Second Prescription

The man who will levigate the root of the giant Asclepias, the Jatamansi, or spikenard (*valeriana Jatamansi*),
Vekhand, the sweet-smelling grass Nagarmotha (*cyperus
pertenuis* or *juncifolius*), and costus with the blood from
a woman's Yoni, and apply it to his forehead, shall ever
be successful in the affairs of love, and shall enjoy a long
course of happiness.

Third Prescription

The man who will take equal parts of Tagar (a flow-
ering plant, *taberna montana* or *coronaria asarobacca*),
of Pimpalimull (the root of *piper dichotomum,* or long
pepper), of Mendha-shinghi (a plant whose fruit is compared with goat-horns or crab-claws), and of Indian
spikenard; mix them together and knead them with
honey, to which is added his Kama-salila, or with any of
the other five Mala (secretions of the body); that man
will find that such a mixture applied to his forehead will
enable him to overcome and subdue the women of the
world.

The following recipe will enable a woman to attract
and preserve her husband's love:

Moisten Gorochana in the blood which appears every

month, and apply it to the forehead as a "Tilak"; as long as it is there and the man looks upon it, so long shall he be in her power.

The following are "Anjan", or magical collyriums for winning love and friendship:

First

Take a human skull from the cemetery or burning ground on the eighth day of the moonlit fortnight of the seventh month Ashvini (September–October), expose it to fire, and collect the soot upon a plate held over it; let this be drawn over the inner surface of the eye-lids, instead of the usual antimony, and the effect will be to fascinate every one.[3]

Second

Take bamboo-manna, Naga-keskar (*messua ferrea*),[4] Korphad (*aloe perfoliata*) and Manshila (red sulphuret of arsenic); reduce them to powder, sift, and use as collyrium; the wearer's eyes will attract the hearts of all.

Third

Take wood of the Tad-palm (toddy-tree), costus, and Tagar-root, levigate in water, and with the latter moisten a piece of silk stuff; convert this into wicks with Shiras-oil, light them and take the soot formed upon a human skull in a cemetery, when held above the lamp; this is a

[3] Nothing in Hindu eyes can be more impure or sacrilegious than such an act as this; the people having, as a rule, the highest reverence for the body from which life has departed. And the horror of the thing is, of course, the secret of its power.

[4] Others translate "Cassia buds."

collyrium which will make every one who looks upon it the servant or slave of the wearer.

Fourth

Take Manshil, Naga-keshar, Kala-umbar (the fruit of *ficus glomerosa*) and bamboo-sugar, and make a collyrium when the Pushya-asterism falls upon a Sunday; its effect will be greatly to increase the mutual love of husband and wife.

The following three prescriptions are powerful in reducing other persons to submission:

First

If a powder made of the Kang, or white panic (*p. italicum*), white Nishottar (*thomea turpethum*), the wing of the Bhramra-bee, costus, lotus flower, and Tagar-root, be thrown upon a man, it will at once have the effect of fascination.

Second

If a powder, made of Vatalu leaves, of Soma-valli (the moon-plant, *asclepias acida,* or *sarcostema viminalis*), and of a garland or rosary placed upon a dead body, and mingled with a little of the man's own Kama-salila, be thrown upon a person, the latter will be surely subdued.

Third

If a powder, made with equal quantities of the Sata-vina-Vrisksha (the "seven-flowered tree", *astonia scholaris* or *echites*), of the Rudraksha (*eleocarpus lanceolatus,* or Ganitrus, a tree sacred to Shiva), and of the seeds of San (Bengal "sun"), be used as before, it will have even a greater effect. This is perhaps the most potent compound for fascinating others.

A Philter-Pill (Vatika)

On any Tuesday, take out the bowels of the blue jay (*coracias indica*), and let some of the fascinator's own Kama-salila be placed inside the body; put the latter into an earthen pot, cover it with a second pot whose bottom must be turned upwards, lute with cloth and clay, and keep in a solitary place for seven days; then take out the contents,[5] pound, reduce to fine powder, make pellets, or pills, and dry them. If one of these be given to a woman, she will be subject to a man, and *vice versa*.

Another Charm

The man who, after enjoying his wife, catches some of his own Kama-salila in his left hand, and applies it to her left foot, will find her entirely submissive to his will.

Another Charm

The woman who before congress will touch with her left foot the Linga of her husband, and will make a practice of this, undoubtedly subdues him, and makes him her slave for life.

Another Charm

Let a man take of the egesta of the spotted-necked pigeon; rock-salt, and the leaves of the Bassia latifolia in equal parts, powder them, and rub the powder upon his Linga before congress, he will become the woman's master.

[5] These, of course, would be putrid in an Indian climate.

Another Charm

Let a man levigate together Kasturi (common musk, also applied to a kind of camphor) and wood of the yellow Tetu-tree; mix them with honey two months old, and apply the substance to his Linga before congress, it will have the same effect.

A Fascinating Incense, or Fumigation

Pound well together sandal-wood, Kunku (red powder prepared from turmeric and alum coloured with lemon-juice and other matters), costus, Krishnaguru (black sanders), Suvasika-puspha (perfumed flowers?), white vala (the fragrant *andropogon muricatum* and the bark of the Deodaru pine; and, after reducing them to fine powder, mix it with honey and thoroughly dry. It is now known as Chintamani-Dhupa, the "thought-mastering incense". If a little of this be used according to the ceremonies prescribed, he who employs it will make all the world submissive to him.

Another Incense

Pound and mix together equal quantities of cardamom-seeds, Olibanum (or gum benzoin), the plant Garur-wel Moon-seed, *monispermum glabrum,* or *cocculus cardifolius,* sandal-wood, the flowers of the eared jasmine, and Bengal madder. This incense is powerful as that above given.

CHAPTER VII

OF DIFFERENT SIGNS IN
MEN AND WOMEN[1]

THE characteristics of a woman whom we should take to wife, are as follows: She should come from a family of equal rank with that of her husband, a house which is known to be valiant and chaste, wise and learned, prudent and patient, correct and becomingly behaved, and famed for acting according to its religion, and for discharging its social duties. She should be free from vices, and endowed with all good qualities, possess a fair face and fine person, have brothers and kinsfolk, and be a great proficient in the Kama-shastra, or Science of Love. Such a girl is truly fitted for marriage; and let a sensible man hasten to take her, by performing the ceremonies which are commanded in the Holy Law.

[1] This chapter has been left in all its original confusion of subjects; it would be easy to order it otherwise; but then it would lose *cachet*.

And here may be learned the marks whereby beauty and good shape of body are distinguished. The maiden whose face is soft and pleasing as the moon; whose eyes are bright and liquid as the fawn's; whose nose is delicate as the sesamum flowers; whose teeth are clean as diamonds and clear as pearls; whose ears are small and rounded; whose neck is like a sea-shell, with three delicate lines or tracings behind; whose lower lip is red as the ripe fruit of the bryony; whose hair is black as the Bhramara's[2] wing; whose skin is brilliant as the flower of the dark-blue lotus, or light as the surface of polished gold; whose feet and hands are red, being marked with the circular Chakra or discus;[3] whose stomach is small, whilst the umbilical region is drawn in; whose shape below the hips is large; whose thighs, being well-proportioned and pleasing as the plantain-tree, make her walk like the elephant, neither too fast nor too slow; whose voice is sweet as the Kokila-bird's—such a girl, especially if her temper be good, her nature kindly, her sleep short and her mind and body not inclined to laziness, should at once be married by the wise man.

But the girl who comes from a bad family; whose body is either very short or very tall, very fat or very thin; whose skin is ever rough and hard; whose hair and eyes are yellowish, the latter like a cat's; whose teeth are long, or are wholly wanting; whose mouth and lips are wide and projecting,[4] with the lower lip of dark colour, and tremulous when speaking; who allows her tongue

[2] The large black bee of Southern Europe, India, etc. Corresponding with the "bumble bee" of England, but without the yellow markings.

[3] Alluded to in a future part of the chapter.

[4] All Easterns uphold the doctrine of the Salernitan School. Noscitur a labiis quantum sit virginis antrum: nocitur a naso quanta sit hasta viro.

to loll out; whose eyebrows are straight; whose temples are depressed; who shows signs of beard, mustachios, and dense body-pile; whose neck is thick; who has some limbs shorter and other longer than the usual proportion; whose one breast is large or high, and the other low or small; whose ears are triangular, like a sifting or winnowing fan; whose second toe is larger and longer than the big toe;[5] whose third toe is blunt, without tip or point, and whose little toes do not touch the ground; whose voice is harsh and laugh is loud; who walks quickly and with uncertain gait; who is full-grown; who is disposed to be sickly, and who bears the name of a mountain (as Govardhan),[6] of a tree (as Anbi), of a river (as Tarangini), of a bird (as Chimani), or of a constellation (as Revati, the 27th lunar mansion)—such a girl, especially if her disposition be irascible and temper violent; if she eat and sleep much; if she be always vexed, troubled and distressed; if her disposition be restless and fidgetty; if she has little understanding in worldly matters; if she be destitute of shame and if her natural disposition be wicked, should be carefully avoided, under all circumstances, by the wise.

So much for the characteristics of the woman. On the other hand, man should be tried, even as gold is tested, in four ways: 1, by the touchstone; 2, by cutting; 3, by heating: and, 4, by hammering. Thus should we take into consideration—1, learning; 2, disposition; 3, quali-

---

[5] In Europe there is much dispute concerning this canon. But the big toe represents the thumb which distinguishes the human from the simian hand, and the longer and the better formed the two are, the higher is the organisation. In this matter races greatly differ: compare, for instance, the short thumb of the Anglo-Saxon with the long thumb of the Celt, or the common Englishman with the common Irishman.

[6] The Hill in Mathura, which Krishna held up in hand.

ties; and 4, action. The first characteristic of a man is courage, with endurance; if he attempt any deed, great or small, he should do it with the spirit of a lion. Second, is prudence: time and place must be determined, and opportunity devised, like the Bak-heron, that stands intently eyeing its prey in the pool below. The third is early rising, and causing others to do the same. The fourth is hardihood in war. The fifth is a generous distribution and division of food and property amongst family and friends. The sixth is duly attending to the wants of the wife. The seventh is circumspection in love matters. The eighth is secrecy and privacy in the venereal act. The ninth is patience and perseverance in all the business of life. The tenth is judgment in collecting and in storing up what may be necessary. The eleventh is not to allow wealth and worldly success to engender pride and vanity, magnificence and ostentation. The twelfth is never aspiring to the unattainable. The thirteenth is contentment with what the man has, if he can get no more. The fourteenth is plainness of diet. The fifteenth is to avoid over-sleep. The sixteenth is to be diligent in the service of employers. The seventeenth is not to fly when attacked by robbers and villains. The eighteenth is working willingly; for instance, not taking into consideration the sun and shade if the labourer be obliged to carry a parcel. The nineteenth is the patient endurance of trouble. The twentieth is to keep the eye fixed upon a great business; and the twenty-first is to study the means properest for success. Now, any person who combines these twenty one qualities is deservedly reputed an excellent man.

When choosing a son-in-law, the following characteristics should be aimed at: He must come from a large family, which has never known sin and poverty. He must be young, handsome, wealthy, brave and influential; diligent in business, moderate in enjoying riches, sweet of speech, well versed in discharging his own duties, known to the world as a mine of virtues, steadfast in mind, and a treasury of mercy, who gives alms and makes charities as far as his means permit. Such a man is described by celebrated poets as a fit person to whom the daughter should be given in marriage.

And these are the defects and blemishes of a son-in-law: The man who is born in a low family, who is vicious, a libertine, pitiless, and ever sickly with dangerous disease, sinful and very wicked, poor and miserly, impotent, prone to conceal the virtues and to divulge the vices of others; a constant traveller, an absentee, one ever away from his home and residing abroad; a debtor, a beggar, a man who has no friendship with the good, or who, if he have it, breaks into quarrel upon trifling things—such a person the wise will not accept as a son-in-law.

We now proceed to the Samudrika-lakshana or chiromantic signs, good and bad, which affect present and future happiness. The length of a man's and woman's life, and the marks which denote it, must first be treated of, because it is useless to see auspicious details if death may shortly be expected. And first of all the palmistry of the man.

Every perfect hand and foot consists of five members, namely the Angushtha (thumb), the Tarjani (forefinger), the Madhyama (middle-finger), the Anamika (ring-finger), and the Kanishthika (little-finger). Now, if an unbroken line in the palm[7] run from the "mount" or base of the little finger, to that of the forefinger, it is a sign that the bearer will live a hundred years. But the man in whose palm an unbroken line runs from the ball or cushion of the little finger to that of the middle finger, should be considered as likely to live for a period of sixty years. Moreover, the man upon whose thumb or chest there is a figure shaped like a barley grain[8], the same will eat bread earned by his own exertions, and he will ever remain happy. As a rule, if the lines in the palms be few, men are poor and penniless; if there be four they are happy; and if more than four, they are threatened with mean and wretched fortunes; moreover, the much streaked palm shows a quarrelsome nature.

The man whose eye is red, whose body is fair and of good complexion likes gold; whose trunk is fleshy and whose arms reach his knees[9], the same will always re-

[7] As a rule the palmistry of the Gypsies is directly derived, like their language, from India, and so artificial a system speaks strongly in favour of a single origin and propagation by tradition. Here, however, the "line of life" (linea vitae) is transferred from the base of the thumb to an unusual place, technically called the Cingulum Veneris.

[8] This figure Europeans turn into an M, and hold to mean marriage. The "barley-mark" in the text seems to correspond with the triangle formed by the "supreme natural Line," the "Line of Life," and the "Line of the Lunar Mount." (Richard Saunders, "Physiognomie and Chiromancie," London, 1671; and "Les mystéres de la Main," Ad. Desbarolles, Paris, Dentu, 1862).

[9] Such was the case with the celebrated Highland cateran, Rob Roy Macgregor.

main rich and enjoy grandeur, opulence, lordship and supremacy.

The man whose thighs are large, will win great wealth; the man whose waist is broad, will be blessed in his wife and many children; the man whose feet are long[10], and whose hands are very delicate, will always enjoy happiness; and the man whose head is large and lengthy[11], will rise to be a prince.

The man whose Linga is very long, will be wretchedly poor. The man whose Linga is very thick, will ever be in distress. The man whose Linga is thin and lean, will be very lucky; and the man whose Linga is short, will be a Rajah.[12] So much concerning the characteristics of men.

And now as regards the other sex. The woman of inauspicious signs, will be or become an orphan, a widow, destitute of brothers and sisters, and without connections, as well as relations, so that her life ends, as it began, in bitterness. Her characteristics, therefore, should be carefully examined before marriage with her is contracted.

Let it be understood that the woman who bears on the sole of her left foot the signs of the Chakra (quoit, peculiar to Vishnu), the Padma (lotus), the Dhvaja (flag),

---

[10] An unusual conformation in the Indian, whose short thin feet are despised by the Afghans, and the adjacent mountaineers. When Ranjit Singh ordered a hundred matchlocks from a celebrated gunsmith across the Indus, he received in return a slipper with a message that the order would be executed as soon as a Sikh's foot could be found to fit that shoe.

[11] An idea long familiar to the world before the days of Dr. Gall.

[12] Here we find a Hindu origin for the naughty schoolboy lines about short and thick—long and thin.

the Chatra (umbrella), the mystical Svastika,[18] and the Kamala, that is, circular lines[14], and not conch-shaped on her finger-tips, that woman will be a Rani (queen). If, however, one or more of these figures be wanting, she will enjoy all the happiness of a crowned head.

The woman who bears on the sole of her left foot a line extending from the "mount" or cushion of the little toe, to the ball of the big toe, that woman will readily obtain a god husband, and will find great happiness in his love.

The woman whose two little toes do not touch the ground whilst walking, will certainly lose her husband; and during her widowhood, she will not be able to keep herself chaste.

The woman whose Tarjani or second toe is the longest of all the toes, will be unchaste even before marriage. What doubt, then, is there of her being an adulteress as long as her youth endures?

The woman whose breasts are fleshy, firm, and handsome, whose bosom is without hair, and whose thighs are like the trunk of an elephant, will enjoy a life of happiness.

The maiden who has black moles upon her left breast, throat and ears, will marry and bear a son having auspi-

---

[18] The Svastika is the crutched cross, known to the Scandinavians as the "hammer of Thor," and supposed to denote the thunderbolt. It is painted on doors in India as an auspicious mark or seal, and is affixed to documents in lieu of signatures by Hindu wives (not widows), who cannot write their names. "Svastika," amongst the Jains, is the emblem of the seventh Guru or spiritual teacher, and the word is also applied to a temple built in the shape of a symbol.

[14] The circular lines being held particularly auspicious.

cious marks; and by her means, all the family will be called blessed.

The maiden whose neck is very long, will be of a wicked and cruel disposition. The maiden whose neck is very short, will be wretchedly poor. The maiden whose neck has three lines or wrinkles, will be of a good disposition, and her lot will be ever fortunate.

The maiden who bears in the palm of her hand lines resembling enclosing walls, and "Toran" or garlands of flowers, and twigs of trees bent into circles[15], will become the wife of a King, although she have been born in a servant's house.

The maiden whose palms have lines in the shape of an Ankush (spiked hook for guiding elephants), a Kuntala (or spur), and a Chakra (quoit or discus), will intermarry with a royal house, and bear a son who shows the most fortunate signs.

It is written in the book Naradokta[16] that marriage should never be contracted with a girl, unless the lines and spots, as interpreted by treatises on Chiromancy, are first examined and found good. The consequence of unauspicious signs is that her birth will cause the death of her father, mother and brother in succession. The man who marries such a maiden, will presently die, and be followed by all his brethren, and these two families will be destroyed.

There are seven kinds of troubles which result from

[15] These ornaments are hung from doorways or about awnings on festive occasions.

[16] That is, the book written by Narada, one of the twenty Rishis or Sages, and a son of Brahma. His name is properly applied to a quarrelsome and embroiling fellow.

having intercourse with the wife of another man. Firstly, adultery shortens or lessens the period of life; secondly, the body becomes spiritless and vigourless; thirdly, the world derides and reproaches the lover; fourthly, he despises himself; fifthly, his wealth greatly decreases; sixthly, he suffers much in this world; and seventhly, he will suffer more in the world to come. Yet, despite all this ignominy, disgrace and contumely, it is absolutely necessary to have connection with the wife of another, under certain circumstances, which will be presently specified.

Great and powerful monarchs have ruined themselves and their realms by their desire to enjoy the wives of others. For instance, in former days the family of the Ravana, King of Lanka (Ceylon), was destroyed because he forcibly abducted Sita, the wife of Rama, and this action gave rise to the Ramayana poem, which is known to the whole world. Vali lost his life for attempting to have connection with Tara, as is fully described in the Kishkinda-kand, a chapter of that history. Kichaka, the Kaurava, together with all his brethren, met with destruction, because he wished to have Draupada[17] (daughter of Drupad), the common wife of the Pandu brothers, as is described in the Viratparvi (section) of the Mahabharat. Such are the destructions which in days past have happened to those who coveted other men's wives; let none, therefore, attempt adultery even in their thoughts.

But there are ten changes in the natural state of men, which require to be taken into consideration. Firstly,

[17] These three represent "Helen of Troy" in the classical history of Hindustan.

when he is in a state of Dhyasa (*desiderium*), at a loss to do anything except to see a particular woman; secondly, when he finds his mind wandering, as if he were about to lose his senses; thirdly, when he is ever losing himself in thought how to woo and win the woman in question; fourthly, when he passes restless nights without the refreshment of sleep; fifthly, when his looks become haggard and his body emaciated; sixthly, when he feels himself growing shameless and departing from all sense of decency and decorum; seventhly, when his riches take to themselves wings and fly; eighthly, when the state of mental intoxication verges upon madness; ninthly, when fainting fits come on; and tenthly, when he finds himself at the door of death.[18]

That these states are produced by sexual passion may be illustrated by an instance borrowed from the history of bygone days. Once upon a time there was a king called Pururava, who was a devout man, and who entered upon such a course of mortification and austerities that Indra, Lord of the Lower Heaven, began to fear lest he himself might be dethroned. The god, therefore, in order to interrupt these penances and other religious acts, sent down from Svarga, his own heaven, Urvashi, the most lovely of the Apsaras (nymphs). The king no sooner saw her than he fell in love with her, thinking day and night of nothing but possessing her, till at last, succeeding in his project, both spent a long time in the pleasures of carnal connection. Presently Indra, happening to remember the Apsara, despatched his messenger, one of the Gandharvas (heavenly minstrels), to the world of mortals, and recalled her. Immediately after her

[18] These ten are the progressive stages of love longing.

departure, the mind of Pururava began to wander; he could no longer concentrate his thoughts upon worship and he felt upon the point of death.

See, then, the state to which that king was reduced by thinking so much about Urvashi! When a man has allowed himself to be carried away captive of desire, he must consult a physician, and the books of medicine which treat upon the subject. And, if he comes to the conclusion that unless he enjoy his neighbour's wife he will surely die, he should, for the sake of preserving his life, possess her once and once only.[19] If, however, there be no such peremptory cause, he is by no means justified in enjoying the wife of another person, merely for the sake of pleasure and wanton gratification.

Moreover, the book of Vatsyayana, the Rishi, teaches us as follows: Suppose that a woman, having reached the lusty vigour of her age, happen to become so inflamed with love for a man, and so heated by passion that she feels herself falling into the ten states before described, and likely to end in death attended with frenzy, if her beloved refuse her sexual commerce. Under these circumstances, the man, after allowing himself to be importuned for a time, should reflect that his refusal will cost her life; he should, therefore, enjoy her on one occasion, but not always.

The following women, however, are absolutely, and under all circumstances, to be excluded from any com-

[19] This was the heathen idea generally, and a friend would hardly have felt justified in refusing, under such circumstances, the loan of his wife. So Seleucus, King of Syria, gave the fair Stratonike to his son, Antiochus, in order to save a life which was endangered by the violence of passion. Equally generous was Socrates, the "Christian before Christianity"; which generosity may, perhaps, account in part for the temper of Xantippe.

merce of the kind. The wife of a Brahman; of a Shrotiya (Brahman learned in the Vedas); of an Agnihotri (priest who keeps up the sacred fire), and of a Puranik (reader of the Puranas). To look significantly at such a woman, or to think of her with a view of sensual desire, is highly improper: what, then, must we think of the sin of carnal couplation with her? In like manner, men prepare to go to Naraka (hell) by lying with the wife of a Khatriya (king, or any man of the warrior caste, now extinct); of a friend or of a relation. The author of this book strongly warns and commands his readers to avoid all such deadly sins.

Indeed, there are certain other women who are never to be enjoyed, however much a man may be tempted. First, a virgin without marrying her; second, a widow[20]; third, a woman living chastely or virtuously with her husband; fourth, the wife of our friend; fifth, the wife of our foe; sixth, any of the reverend women specified above; seventh, the wife of a pupil or a disciple; eighth, a woman born in one's own family; ninth, a woman who has been defiled; tenth, a mad woman; eleventh, a woman older than one's self[21]; twelfth, the wife of a Guru, spiritual tutor, instructor or guide; thirteenth,

[20] Because by Hindu custom, if not by the old law, the lover cannot marry a widow.

[21] Easterns are all agreed upon this point, and the idea is that the embraces of a woman older than the husband, "burn" and destroy his strength. It is certain that when there is a considerable difference of age, the younger of the two suffers in appearance, if not in health. How many women we see in civilized countries with that young-old look, which at once assures the observer that they are married to men much their seniors? We seldom meet in society with the reverse case, for ridicule always attaches to a man's marrying a woman whose age greatly execeeds his own. Yet the few instances which appear justify our belief that there is something the reverse of hygienic in the practice.

one's mother-in-law; fourteenth, one's maternal aunt (mother's sister); fifteenth, the wife of one's maternal uncle[22]; sixteenth, one's paternal aunt (father's sister); seventeenth, one's paternal uncle's wife; eighteenth, a sister; nineteenth, a pregnant woman; twentieth, a woman with whom one is not acquainted; twenty-first, a woman who has committed mortal sins and crimes; twenty-second, a woman whose complexion is entirely yellow; twenty-third, a woman whose complexion is quite black. It is laid down in the Shastras (scriptures) that the wise should never, under any circumstances, have connection with these twenty-three kinds of women, as well as with others, bearing any relationship to one.

The following is a list of the women who serve but as go-betweens[23]: First, a gardener's wife. Second, a woman who is a personal friend. Third, a widow. Fourth, a nurse. Fifth, a dancing-girl. Sixth, a woman engaged in manual or mechanical arts. Seventh, a woman hired as a servant or maid to the women of the family. Eighth, an attendant as distinguished from a slave girl. Ninth, a woman who goes from house to house speaking sweet words. Tenth, a woman with whom we can talk freely about love and enjoyment. Eleventh, a young woman under sixteen. Twelfth, a female ascetic or mendicant in the name of religion.

[22] In Sanskrit, and in the Prakrit or modern language of Hindostan, there are different names for our "aunt" Mavashi, for instance, is the maternal aunt, and Mami, the maternal uncle's wife.

[23] This need not necessarily be taken in a bad sense, as "procuress". In Hindu, as well as in Muslim families, women are sufficiently secluded to require the assistance of feminine Mercuries in matters of marriage.

Thirteenth, a woman who sells milk and buttermilk. Fourteenth, a tailoress. Fifteenth, a woman fit to be called "Mistress Grandmother". The amorous should prefer these kind of persons, as, when deputed upon such messages, they do their work kindly and well.

The following is a list of the women who can most easily be subdued.[24] First, a woman whose deportment shows signs of immodesty. Second, a widow. Third, a woman who is highly accomplished in singing, in playing musical instruments, and in similar pleasant arts. Fourth, a woman who is fond of conversation. Fifth, a woman steeped in poverty. Sixth, the wife of an imbecile or an impotent person. Seventh, the wife of a fat and tun-bellied man. Eighth, the wife of a cruel and wicked man. Ninth, the wife of one who is shorter than herself. Tenth, the wife of an old man. Eleventh, the wife of a very ugly man. Twelfth, a woman accustomed to stand in the doorway and to stare at passers-by. Thirteenth, women of variable disposition. Fourteenth, the barren woman, especially if she and her husband desire the blessing of issue. Fifteenth, the woman who brags and boasts. Sixteenth, the woman who has long been separated from her husband, and deprived of her natural refreshment. Seventeenth, the woman who has never learned the real delight of carnal copulation;[25] and eighteenth, the woman whose mind remains girlish.

[24] This can hardly be used in an honest sense: it might be translated "seduced," were not that word so liable to misuse and misconstruction. What man in his senses can believe in the "seduction" of a married woman? As a rule, indeed, the seduction is all on the other side.

[25] Which, allow us to state, is the case with most English women and a case to be remedied only by constant and intelligent study of the Ananga Ranga Scripture.

And now to describe the signs and symptoms by which we are to know when women are enamoured of us. Firstly, that woman loves a man when she is not ashamed of looking at him,[26] and of boldly and without fear or deference keeping her eyes fixed upon his. Secondly, when she moves her foot to and fro whilst standing up, and draws, as it were, lines upon the ground. Thirdly, when she scratches divers limbs without sufficient reason. Fourthly, when she leers, looks obliquely, and casts side glances. Fifthly, when she laughs causelessly at the sight of a man.

And furthermore, the woman who, instead of answering a straightforward question, replies by joking and jesting words; who slowly and deliberately follows us wherever we go; who, under some pretext or other, dwells upon our faces or forms with a wistful and yearning glance; who delights in walking before us and displaying her legs or her bosom; who behaves to us with a mean and servile submission, ever praising and flattering; who contracts friendships with our friends and who is ever asking them, "In the house of such and such a person, are there any wives? Does he love them much? And are they very beautiful?" Who, looking towards us, sings a sweet air; who passes her hands frequently over her breasts and her arms; who cracks her fingers; who yawns and sighs when not expected to do so; who will never appear before us, though we call and summon her, unless in her most becoming dress;

---

[26] In the East, women take the first step in such matters. Nothing can be more ridiculous than to see the bearded and turbaned Turk blushing, "boggling," and looking silly as he is being inspected by a pair of bold feminine eyes.

who throws flowers and similar articles upon us; who, pretexting various things, often goes into and comes forth from the house; and finally, whose face, hands, and feet break into perspiration when she casually sees us; that woman showing any such signs and symptoms, is enamoured of us, and is strongly excited by passion; all we have to do, if versed in the art of love, is to send an able go-between.

On the other hand, the following women are hard to be subdued: First, the wife who is full of love for her husband. Second, the woman whose cold desires and contempt for congress keep her chaste. Third, the woman who is envious of another's prosperity and success. Fourth, the mother of many children. Fifth, a dutiful daughter or daughter-in-law. Sixth, a courteous and respectful woman. Seventh, a woman who fears and stands in awe of her parents and those of her husband. Eighth, a wealthy woman, who ever suspects and often wrongly, that we love her money better than herself. Ninth, a woman who is shy, bashful, and retiring in the presence of strangers. Tenth, an avaricious and covetous woman. Eleventh, a woman who has no avarice or covetousness. Such women are not easily secured, nor is it worth our while to waste our hours in pursuing them.

The following are the places where a woman should not be enjoyed: First, the place where fire is lighted with the religious formula Agni-mukha and other Mantras. Second, in the presence of a Brahman or any other reverend man. Third, under the eyes of an aged person, to whom respect is due, as a Guru (spiritual guide), or a father. Fourth, when a great man is looking on. Fifth, by the side of a river or any murmuring stream. Sixth, at a Panwata, a place erected for drawing water from wells, tanks and so forth. Seventh, in a temple dedicated to the gods. Eighth, in a fort or castle. Ninth, in a guard-room, police-station, or in any government place where prisoners are confined. Tenth, on a highway. Eleventh, in a house of another person. Twelfth, in the forest. Thirteenth, in an open place, such as a meadow or an upland. Fourteenth, on ground where men are buried or burned. The consequences of carnal connection at such places are always disastrous; they breed misfortunes, and, if children are begotten, these turn out bad and malicious persons.

The following are the times when women are not to be enjoyed: First, by day, unless their class and temperament require coition during the light hours. Second, during or at the Sankranti-parvani, that is to say, when the sun or a planet passes from one side of the zodiac to another.[27] Third, during the Sharad, or cold season[28] (October to November). Fourth, during the Grishma, or hot season[29] (June to July). Fifth, in the Amavasya (the last, the thirtieth, or the new moon day of the Hindu month), unless the Love-shastra specify the contrary. Sixth, during the periods when the man's body suffers from fever. Seventh, during the time of a "Vrata"

[27] Parvani (Sanskrit Parva), is applied to certain times, such as the solstices and the equinoxes, when good actions are most acceptable.

[28] It must be remembered that during the whole period of the sun's southing (Dakshanayana, opposed to Uttarayana, or his northerly direction), the high-caste Hindu will not marry.

[29] The other four are Vasanta, or spring (April to May); Varsha, the rains (August to September); Hermanta, or the cold season (December to January); and Shishira, early spring (February to March). Thus the Hindu year contains six Ritu or seasons.

any self-imposed religious observance, with obligation to carry it out. Eighth, in the evening time; and ninth, when wearied with warfare. The consequences of congress at such epochs are as disastrous as if the act took place in a prohibited spot.

The following is the situation which the wise men of old have described as being best fitted for sexual intercourse with women. Choose the largest, and finest, and the most airy room in the house, purify it thoroughly with whitewash, and decorate its spacious and beautiful walls with pictures and other objects upon which the eye may dwell with delight.[30] Scattered about this apartment place musical instruments, especially the pipe and the lute; with refreshments, as cocoa-nut, betel-leaf and milk, which is so useful for retaining and restoring vigour; bottles of rose water and various essences, fans and chauris for cooling the air, and books containing amorous songs, and gladdening the glance with illustrations of love-postures. Splendid Divalgiri, or wall lights, should gleam around the wall, reflected by a hundred mirrors, whilst both man and woman should contend against any reserve, or false shame, giving themselves up in complete nakedness to unrestrained voluptuousness, upon a high and handsome bedstead, raised on tall legs, furnished with many pillows, and covered by a rich chatra, or canopy; the sheets being besprinkled with flowers and the coverlet scented by burning luscious

---

[30] This precaution might be adopted in modern civilization. It was practised by the Greeks and Romans, for the purpose of begetting graceful and beautiful children; and, considering the history of mothermarks and other puerperal curiosities, we should be careful how we determine that the conception cannot be favourably, as well as unfavourably influenced by the aspect of objects around the parents.

incense, such as aloes and other fragrant woods.[31] In such a place, let the man, ascending the throne of love, enjoy the woman in ease and comfort, gratifying his and her every wish and every whim.

[31] Concerning the effect of perfumes upon the organs, see Chapter IX.

CHAPTER VIII

TREATING OF EXTERNAL ENJOYMENTS

By "external enjoyments" are meant the processes which should always precede internal enjoyment or coition. The wise have said that before congress, we must develop the desire of the weaker sex through certain preliminaries, which are many and various; such as the various embraces and kisses; the Nakhadana, or unguiculations; the Dashanas, or morsications; the Keshagrahanas, or manipulating the hair, and other amorous blandishments. These affect the senses and divert the mind from coyness and coldness. After which tricks and toyings, the lover will proceed to take possession of the place.

There are eight Alinganas, or modes of embracing

which will here be enumerated and carefully described:[1]

1. Vrikshadhirudha is the embrace which simulates the climbing of a tree,[2] and it is done as follows: When the husband stands up the wife should place one foot upon his foot,[3] and raise the other leg to the height of his thigh, against which she presses it. Then encircling his waist with her arms, even as a man prepares to swarm up a palm-trunks, she holds and presses him forcibly, bends her body over his, and kisses him as if sucking the water of life.

2. Tila-Tandula, the embrace which represents the mixture of sesamum-seed with husked rice (Tandul). The man and woman, standing in front of each other, should fold each other to the bosom by closely encircling the waist. Then taking care to remain still, and by no means to move, they should approach the Linga to the Yoni, both being veiled by the dress, and avoid interrupting the contact for some time.

3. Lalatika, so called because forehead (lalata) touches forehead. In this position great endearment is shown

---

[1] The Alinganas are illustrated in almost every edition of "Koka Pandit," and so are the broader subjects treated of in the following chapter. At Puna (Poonah) and other parts of Western India, there are artists who make this the business of their lives, and who sell a series of about eighty body colours, at the rate of two to five Rupees each. The treatment is purely conventional, and the faces, as well as the dresses, probably date from several centuries ago. A change took place when an unhappy Anglo-Indian Officer, wishing to send home a portrait of his wife, applied to one of our artists with that admirably naïve ignorance of everything "native," which is the growing custom of his race. The result was that the Englishwoman's golden hair and beautiful features appear in some fifty or sixty highly compromising attitudes, and will continue to do so for many a generation to come.

[2] Compare the slang word in French, "grimper".

[3] Both feet being, of course, naked.

by the close pressure of arms round the waist, both still standing upright, and by the contact of brow, cheek, and eyes, of mouth, breasts, and stomach.

4. Jaghan-alingana, meaning "hips, loins, and thighs." In this embrace the husband sits[4] upon the carpet and the wife upon his thighs, embracing and kissing him with fond affection. In returning her fondling, her Lungaden, or petticoats, are raised, so that her Lungi, or under-garments, may come in contact with his clothes, and her hair is thrown into the dishevelled state, symbolizing passion; or the husband, for variety's sake, may sit upon the wife's lap.

5. Viddhaka, when the nipples touch the opposite body. The husband sits still, closing his eyes, and the wife, placing herself close to him, should pass her right arm over his shoulder and apply her bosom to his, pressing him forcibly, whilst he returns her embrace with equal warmth.

6. Urupagudha, so called from the use of the thighs. In this embrace both stand up, passing their arms round each other, and the husband places his wife's legs between his own so that the inside of his thighs may come in contact with the outside of hers. As in all cases, kissing must be kept up from time to time. This is a process peculiar to those who are greatly enamoured of each other.

7. Dughdanir-alingana, or the "milk and water embrace," also called "Kshiranira," with the same signification. In this mode the husband lies upon the bed, resting

[4] Sitting invariably means cross-legged, like a tailor upon his board, or at squat, like a bird, and the seat is a mat, or carpet, in India, and a divan in the nearer East.

on one side, right or left; the wife throws herself down near him with her face to his, and closely embraces him, the members and limbs of both touching, and entangled, as it were, with the corresponding parts of the other. And thus they should remain until desire is thoroughly aroused in both.

8. Valleri-vreshtita, or "embracing as the creeper twines about the tree", is performed as follows: Whilst both are standing upright, the wife clings to her husband's waist, and passes her leg around his thigh, kissing him repeatedly and softly until he draws in his breath like one suffering from the cold. In fact, she must endeavour to imitate the vine enfolding the tree which supports it.

Here end the embracements; they should be closely studied, followed up by proper intelligence of the various modes of kisses, which must accompany and conclude the Alinganas. And understand at once that there are seven places highly proper for osculation, in fact, where all the world kisses. These are: First, the lower lip. Second, both the eyes. Third, both the cheeks. Fourth, the head.[5] Fifth, the mouth. Sixth, both breasts; and seventh, the shoulders. It is true that the people of certain countries have other places, which they think proper to kiss; for instance, the voluptuaries of Satadesha have adopted the following formula:

But this is far from being customary with the men of our country or of the world in general.

---

[5] In Europe, osculation upon the head and forehead is a paternal salutation, and, as a rule, men kiss one another upon both cheeks, and only their wives and concubines on the mouth. These distinctions are ignored by Orientals.

Furthermore, there are ten different kinds of kisses, each of which has its own and proper name, and these will be described in due order.

1. Mlita-kissing, which means "mishrita", mixing or reconciling. If the wife be angry, no matter however little, she will not kiss the face of her husband; the latter then should forcibly fix his lips upon hers and keep both mouths united till her ill-temper passes away.

2. Sphurita-kissing, which is connected with twitching and vellication. The wife should approach her mouth to that of her husband, who then kisses her lower lip, whilst she draws it aways, jerking, as it were, without any return of osculation.

3. Ghatika, or neck-nape kissing, a term frequently used by the poets. This is done by the wife, who, excited with passion, covers her husband's eyes with her hands, and closing her own eyes, thrusts her tongue into his mouth, moving it to and fro with a motion so pleasant and slow that it at once suggests another and higher form of enjoyment.

4. Tiryak, or oblique kissing. In this form the husband, standing behind or at the side of his wife, places his hand beneath her chin, catches hold of it and raises it, until he has made her face look up to the sky;[6] then he takes her lower lip beneath his teeth, gently biting and chewing it.

5. Uttaroshtha, or "upper-lip kissing". When the wife

[6] A fair specimen of the verbosity of Hindu style, which is so seldom realized or copied by Europeans speaking "native" languages. We should say "hold her chin and raise her face," or, to quote Ovid's Metamorphoses, "ad lumina lumen"—Attollens, which the Hindu would only half understand. This remark might be illustrated at considerable length.

is full of desire, she should take her husband's lower lip between her teeth, chewing and biting it gently; whilst he does the same to her upper lip. In this way both excite themselves to the height of passion.

6. Pindita, or "lump-kissing". The wife takes hold of her husband's lips with her fingers, passes her tongue over them and bites them.

7. Samputa, or "casket-kissing". In this form the husband kisses the inside mouth of his wife, whilst she does the same to him.

8. Hanuvatra-kissing.[7] In this mode the kiss should not be given at once, but begin with moving the lips towards one another in an irritating way, with freaks, pranks, and frolics. After toying together for some time, the mouths should be advanced, and the kiss exchanged.

9. Pratibodha, or "awakening kiss". When the husband, who has been absent for some time, returns home and finds his wife sleeping upon the carpet in a solitary bedroom, he fixes his lips upon hers, gradually increasing the pressure until such time as she awakes. This is by far the most agreeable form of osculation, and it leaves the most pleasant of memories.

10. Samaushtha-kissing. This is done by the wife taking the mouth and lips of the husband into hers, pressing them with her tongue, and dancing about him as she does so.

Here end the sundry forms of kisses. And now must be described the various ways of Nakhadana, that is, of titillating and scratching with the nails. As it will not be understood what places are properest for this kind of dalliance, it should be explained as a preliminary

[7] In Sanskrit, "Hanu" means jaw.

that there are eleven parts upon which pressure may be exerted with more or less force. These are: First, the neck. Second, the hands. Third, both thighs. Fourth, both breasts. Fifth, the back. Sixth, the sides. Seventh, both axillæ. Eighth, the whole chest or bosom. Ninth, both hips. Tenth, the Mons Veneris and all the parts about the Yoni; and, eleventh, both the cheeks.

Furthermore, it is necessary to learn the times and seasons when this style of manipulation is advisable. These are: First, when there is anger in the mind of the woman. Second, at the time of first enjoying her or of taking her virginity. Third, when going to separate for a short time. Fourth, when about journeying to a foreign and distant country. Fifth, when a great pecuniary loss has been sustained. Sixth, when excited with desire of congress; and, seventh, at the season of Virati, that is to say, when there is no Rati, or furor venereus.[8] At such times the nails should always be applied to the proper places.

The nails, when in good condition and properest for use, are without spots[9] and lines, clean, bright, convex,[10] hard, and unbroken. Wise men have given in the Shastras these six qualities of the nails.

There are seven different ways of applying the nails,

[8] "Virati" usually signifies being freed or refraining from carnal and worldly desires and passions; the extinction of earthly affections, and so forth.

[9] The Hindus do not appear to have any special superstition about the white spots on the nails, which the vulgar of Europe call "gifts," because they portend presents.

[10] Some wrongly translate this word "growing," or increasing. It means convex; in fact, what we call "filbert nails," opposed to the flat, the concave, and the spatulated.

which may be remembered by the Mandalaka or oblong formula on the following page:

1. Chúrit-nakhadana is setting the nails in such a way upon the cheeks, lower lip and breasts, without leaving any marks, but causing horripilation, till the woman's body-hair bristles up, and a shudder passes all over the limbs.[11]

2. Ardhachandra-nakhadana is effected by impressing with the nails upon the neck and breasts a curved mark, which resembles a half-moon (Ardhachandra).

3. Mandalaka is applying the nails to the face for some time, and indeed until a sign is left upon it.

4. Tarunabhava or Rekha (a line) is the name given by men conversant with the Kamashastra to nail-marks longer than two or three finger-breadths on the woman's head, thighs and breasts.

5. The Mayurapada ("peacock's foot" or claw) is made by placing the thumb upon the nipple, and the four fingers upon the breast adjacent, at the same time pressing the nails till the mark resembles the trail of the peacock, which he leaves when walking upon mud.

6. Shasha-pluta, or the "hooping of a hair", is the mark made upon the darker part of the breast when no other portion is affected.

7. Anvartha-nakhadana is a name applied to the three deep marks or scratches made by the nails of the first

[11] The European superstition is, that when horripilation takes place without apparent cause, a person is passing over the spot where the shudderer will be buried. This idea can hardly exist amongst a people who sensibly burn their dead in fixed places, far removed from the haunts of the living; and amongst Muslims, as well as Hindus, the "goose flesh," as we call it in our homely way, is a sign of all the passions.

three fingers on the back, the breasts and the parts about the Yoni. This Nakhadana or unguiculation is highly proper when going abroad to a distant country, as it serves for a keep-sake and a token of remembrance.

The voluptuary, by applying the nails as above directed with love and affection, and driven wild by the fury of passion, affords the greatest comfort to the sexual desires of the woman; in fact, there is nothing, perhaps, which is more delightful to both husband and wife than the skilful use of unguiculation.

Furthermore, it is advisable to master the proper mode of morsication or biting. It is said by persons who are absorbed in the study of sexual intercourse, that the teeth should be used to the same places where the nails are applied with the exception, however, of the eyes, the upper lip, and the tongue. Moreover, the teeth should be pressed until such time as the woman begins to exclaim, Hu! hu![12] after which enough has been done.

The teeth to be preferred in the husband, are those whose colour is somewhat rosy,[13] and not of a dead white; which are bright and clean, strong, pointed and short, and which form close and regular rows. On the other hand, those are bad which are dingy and unclean, narrow, long and projecting forward, as though they would leave the mouth.[14]

[12] This interjection usually denotes grief or pain, and here perhaps it is used in the latter sense.

[13] "Rosy teeth" suggest a resemblance to our "curly teeth," popularly associated with straight hair. The author, however, is right according to the most modern and the best authorities, in asserting that dead white is a bad colour, liable to caries, and easily tarnishing.

[14] Prognathism and Macrodontism are unknown to the higher castes of Hindus.

Like the unguiculations, there are seven different Dashanas or ways of applying the teeth, which may be remembered by the following Mandalaka or oblong formula:[15]

1. Gudhaka-dashana, or "secret biting", is applying the teeth only to the inner or red part[16] of the woman's lip, leaving no outside mark so as to be seen by the world.

2. Uchun-dashana, the wise tell us, is the word applied to biting any part of a woman's lips or cheeks.

3. Pravalamani-dashana, or "coral biting", is that wonderful union of the man's tooth and the woman's lips, which converts desire into a burning flame; it cannot be described, and is to be accomplished only by long experience, not by the short practice of a few days.

4. Bindu-dashana ("dot" or "drop-biting") is the mark left by the husband's two front teeth upon the woman's lower lip, or upon the place where the Tilla or brow-mark is worn.

5. Bindu-mala (a "rosary", or "row of dots" or "drops"), is the same as the preceding, except that all the front teeth are applied, so as to form a regular line of marks.

6. Khandabhrak is the cluster or multitude of impressions made by the prints of the husband's teeth upon the brow and cheek, the neck and breast of the wife. If disposed over the body like the Mandalaka, or Dashanagramandal, the mouth-shaped oblong traced above, it will greatly add to her beauty.

[15] Also called Dashanagramandal or circle of the principal bitings.
[16] The darker Hindus, like Africans, do not show redness in the lips, and the Arabs, curious to say, exceedingly admire brown lips.

7. Kolacharcha is the name given by the wise to the deep and lasting marks of his teeth which the husband, in the heat of passion, and in the grief of departure when going to a foreign land, leaves upon the body of his wife. After his disappearance, she will look at them, and will frequently remember him with yearning heart.

So far for the styles of morsication. And now it is advisable to study the different fashions of Keshagrahana, or manipulating the hair, which, upon a woman's head, should be soft, close, thick, black, and wavy, not curled, nor straight.

One of the best ways of kindling hot desire in a woman is, at the time of rising, softly to hold and handle the hair, according to the manner of doing so laid down in the Kamashastra.

The Keshagrahana are of four kinds, which may be remembered by the

1. Samahastakakeshagrahana, or "holding the hair with both hands", is when the husband encloses it between his two palms behind his wife's head, at the same time kissing her lower lip.

2. Tarangarangakeshagrahana, or "kissing the hair in wavy (or sinuous) fashion", is when the husband draws his wife towards him by the back hair, and kisses her at the same time.

3. Bhujangavallika, or the "dragon's turn",[17] is when the husband, excited by the approaching prospect of sexual congress, amorously seizes the hind knot of his wife's hair, at the same time closely embracing her. This is done in a standing position, and the legs should

[17] Bhujanga is a dragon, a cobra, a snake generically, or a man who keeps a mistress.

be crossed with one another. It is one of the most exciting of all toyings.

4. Kamavatansakeshagrahana, or "holding the crest-hair of love",[18] is when, during the act of copulation, the husband holds with both hands his wife's hair above her ears, whilst she does the same thing to him, and both exchange frequent kisses upon the mouth.

Such, then, are the external enjoyments described in the due order according to which they ought to be practised. Those only are mentioned which are well known to, and are highly appreciated by the world. There are many others by no means so popular, and these are omitted, lest this treatise become an unwieldy size.[19] The following may, however, be mentioned:

The blandishments of love are a manner of battle, in which the stronger wins the day. And in order to assist us in the struggle, there are two forms of attack, known as Karatadana and Sitkreutoddesha.

[18] Avatansa means a crest, a tuft, or an earring.

[19] The reader will remember that the Hindus, as a rule, are a race of vegetarians, who rarely drink any stimulant such as wine, ale and spirits, or even tea, coffee and chocolate. They look with horror upon the meat-eater, that makes his body a grave for the corpses of animals; and they attach a bad name to all narcotics except tobacco, leaving opium and Bhang or Hashish to low fellows and ribald debauchees. It is evident that, under such circumstances, their desires, after the first heat of youth, will be comparatively cold, and that both sexes, especially the weaker, require to be excited by a multitude and a variety of preliminaries to possession, which would defeat their own object in case of Europeans. Thus also we may account for their faith in pepper, ginger, cloves, cinnamon, and other spices which go by the name of "Garm Masala," or hot condiments; these would have scanty effect upon the beef-eating and beer-bibbing Briton, but they exert a sufficiently powerful action upon a people of water-drinkers and rice or pulse-feeders.

Karatadana, as the word denotes,[20] are soft tappings and pattings with the hand, by the husband or the wife, upon certain members of each other's persons. And in this process there are four divisions, which the man applies to the woman:

1. Prasritahasta, or patting with the open palm.

2. Uttanyahasta, the same reversed; done with the back of the hand.

3. Mushti, or striking gently with the lower or fleshy part of the closed hand; softly hammering, as it were.

4. Sampatahasta, or patting with the inner part of the hand, which is slightly hollowed for the purpose, like the cobra's hood.

And here may be specified the several members that should thus be operated upon. First, the flesh below the ribs, with No. 1. Second the Mons Veneris and vicinity of the Yoni; also with No. 1. Third, the bosom and breasts, with No. 2. Fourth, the back and hip, with No. 3. Fifth, the head with No. 4.

There are also four corresponding divisions of the practices used by the woman to the man:

1. Santanika, a name given by learned men to the act of a wife gently patting with the closed fist her husband's breast when the two have become one, so as to increase his pleasure.

2. Pataka is when the wife, also during congress, pats her husband gently with the open hand.

3. Bindumala is the name given only by men when the wife, at the time of coition, fillips her husband's body with the thumbs only.

4. Kundala is the name given by the older poets when

20 "Kara," a hand, and Tadana, "striking."

93

the wife, during copulation, fillips her husband's body with thumb and fore-finger, not with the rest of the hand.

And now of the Sitkriti, or inarticulate sound produced by drawing in the breath between the closed teeth; these are the peculiar privilege and prerogative of women, and the wise divide them into five kinds:

1. Hinkriti is the deep and grave sound, like "Hun! hun! hun!", or "Hin! hin! hin!"[21] produced in the nose and mouth with the slightest use of the former member.

2. Stanita is the low rumbling, like distant thunder, expressed by "Ha! ha!" or by "Han! han! han!" produced by the throat without the concurrence of the nasal muscles.

3. Sitkriti is the expiration or emission of breath, like the hissing of a serpent, expressed by "Shan! shan!" or "Shish! shish!" and produced only in the mouth.

4. Utkriti is the cracking sound, resembling the splitting of a bamboo, expressed by "T'hat! t'hat!" and formed by applying the tongue-tip to the palate,[22] and by moving it as rapidly as possible, at the same time pronouncing the interjection.

5. Bhavakriti is a rattling sound, like the fall of heavy rain-drops, expressed by "T'hap! t'hap!" produced by the lips: but it can be produced only at the time of congress.

These several Sitkritis in the woman's mouth at the moment of enjoyment, will respectively resemble the cry of the quail (Lava), of the Indian cuckoo (Kokila),

[21] In all these interjections, the terminal liquid is a highly nasalized nunnation.

[22] Somewhat in the same way as an Englishman urges on a horse.

of the spotted-necked pigeon (Kapota), of the Hansa-goose and of the peacock. The sounds should especially be produced when the husband kisses, bites, and chews his wife's lower lip; and the sweetness of the utterance greatly adds to enjoyment, and promotes the congress of the sexual act.

Furthermore, be it known to men the peculiar characteristics of the Ashtamahanayika, or the eight great forms of Nayika:[23]

1. Khanditanayika, when the husband bears upon his body all the marks of sexual enjoyment, produced by sleeping with a rival wife; and when, with eyes reddened by keeping late hours, he returns to his beloved struck with fear and in an agitated state, coaxing her, and speaking sweet words, for the purpose of sueing her to congress, and she half listens to him, but yields at last. Such is the name given to her by the great poets of the olden time.

2. Vasakasajjita is the word applied by the learned to the wife, who, having spread a soft, fine bed, in a charming apartment, sits upon it at night-time, and awaits her husband, with great expectation, now half closing her eyes, then fixing her glance on the door.

3. Kalakantarita, say wise men, is the term of a wife, who when her husband, after grossly injuring her, falls at her feet and begs for pardon, answers him loudly and in great wrath, drives him from her presence, and determines not to see him again; but presently, waxing

[23] A mistress, or one beloved, the feminine of Nayak, meaning the head, a chief, the lover, the hero of a play, or the best gem in a necklace; hence the corrupted word "Naik," a corporal in the "native" army.

repentant, laments in various ways the pains and sorrows of separation, and at last recovers quietude by the hope of reunion.

4. Abhisarika is the woman whose sexual passions being in a state of overflowing, dresses herself, and goes forth shamelessly and wantonly at night-time to the house of some strange man, in the hope of carnal copulation with him.

5. Vipralabdha is the disappointed woman, who, having sent a go-between to some strange man, appointing him to meet her a certain place, repairs there, confused and agitated with the prospect of congress, but sees the go-between returning alone, and without the lover, which throws her into a state of fever.

6. Viyogini is the melancholy woman, who, during the absence of her husband in a far country, smells the fragrant and exciting perfumes[24] of sandalwood, and other odorous substances, and looking upon the lotus-flower and the moonlight, falls into a passion of grief.

7. Svadhinapurvapatika is the name given to the wife whose husband instead of gratifying her amorous desires, and studying her carnal wants, engages in the pursuit of philosophic knowledge derived from meditation.

8. Utkanthita, according to the best poets, is the woman who loves her husband very dearly, whose eyes are light and lively, who has decorated herself with jewels and garlands, well knowing the wishes of her

[24] There are many theories upon this subject in the East. For instance, the Narcissus-flower is everywhere supposed to excite the woman and depress the man, whilst the Mimosa blossom gives an essence which the Arabs call "Fitnah," trouble or revolt, because its action is direct and powerful upon the passions of their wives as the Spanish "Viento de las mujeres."

man, and who, burning with desire, awaits his coming,
propped up with pillows in a sleeping-apartment appro-
priated to pleasure, and sumptuously adorned with mirrors and pictures.[25]

[25] These eight Nayikas are borrowed from the language of the
Hindu drama.

CHAPTER IX

TREATING OF INTERNAL ENJOYMENTS IN ITS VARIOUS FORMS

By "internal enjoyment" is meant the art of congress which follows the various external preliminaries described in the last chapter. These embraces, kisses and sundry manipulations, must always be practised according to the taste of husband and wife, and if persisted in as the Shastra directs, they will excessively excite the passions of the woman, and will soften and loosen her Yoni so as to be ready for carnal connection.

The following verses show how much art and science there is in a matter which appears so simple to the uneducated and vulgar.

"What is the remedy when a woman is mightier than a man? Although she be very strong, yet no sooner are her legs placed wide apart, than she loses her force of passion, and is satisfied."

"Thus the Yoni from being tight and compact, becomes slack and loose; let the husband, therefore, press her thighs together, and she will be equally able to struggle with him at the time of congress."

"Well, if a woman be only twelve or thirteen years old, and the man is quite grown up, and has lost the first vigour of his youth, what must be done to make them equal?"

"In such a case, the legs of the woman must be stretched out to the fullest extent, so as to weaken the powers, and by these means the man will prove himself her equal."

There are five main Bandha or A'sana—forms or postures of congress—which appear in the following shape,
and each of these will require its own description successively, and in due order.[1]

(A) Uttana-bandha (*i.e.*, supine posture) is the great

[1] The reader will bear in mind that the exceeding pliability of the Hindu's limbs enables him to assume attitudes absolutely impossible to the European, and his chief object in congress is to avoid tension of the muscles, which would shorten the period of enjoyment. For which reason, even in the act of love, he will delay to talk, to caress his wife, to eat, drink, chew Pan-supari, and perhaps smoke a water-pipe.

Stripped of its excessive verbiage, the Hindu "façon de faire," are simple enough. The five great divisions represent: 1. The woman lying supine (upon her back); 2. Lying on her side (right or left); 3. Sitting in various ways; 4. Standing, or as the vulgar call an upright; and, lastly, 5. Lying prone (upon breast and stomach). Of the first division, there are eleven subdivisions; of the second, three; of the third, ten; of the fourth, three; and two of the fifth class, making a total of twenty-nine, and with three forms of Puruhayit, a grand total of thirty-two.

As in similar European treatises, the Kamashastra is very brief and unsatisfactory, except in the principal positions, and it can hardly be understood without illustrations. Some appear to be identical with division so-called by men well versed in the Art of Love, when a woman lies upon her back, and her husband sits close to her upon his hams. But is this all that can be said of it? No! no! there are eleven sub-divisions, as shown in the table on the following page.

And now of the several sub-divisions:

1. Samapada-uttana-bandha, is when the husband places his wife upon her back, raises both her legs, and placing them upon his shoulders, sits close to her and enjoys her.

2. Nagara-uttana-bandha, is when the husband places his wife upon her back, sits between her legs, raises them both, keeping them on either side of his waist, and thus enjoys her.

3. Traivikrama-uttana-bandha, is when one of the wife's legs is left lying upon the bed or carpet, the other being placed upon the head of the husband, who supports himself upon both hands. This position is very admirable.

4. Vyomapada-uttana-bandha, is when the wife, lying upon her back, raises with her hands both legs, drawing them as far back as her hair; the husband, then sitting close to her, places both hands upon her breasts and enjoys her.

---

others, at least no distinction can be learnt from the text. Moreover, it is evident that the Yoni of the Hindu woman must be placed exceptionally high, ortherwise many of the postures would be quite impossible—these varieties of conformation are exceedingly interesting to the ethnologist, but the matter is far too extensive for discussing here. The subject of constricting the Yoni is also ethnologically of great importance, as will be seen when the reader arrives at the paragraph. An allusion has already been made to the Hindu practice of affecting conception by both parents looking at pictures of noble and beautiful forms; a custom well-known to the ancients, but now unaccountably neglected. (See Chapter VIII.)

5. Smarachakrasana, or the position of the Kama's wheel, a mode very much enjoyed by the voluptuary. In this form, the husband sits between the legs of his wife, extends his arms on both sides of her as far as he can, and thus enjoys her.

6. Avidarita is that position when the wife raises both her legs, so that they may touch the bosom of her husband, who, sitting between her thighs, embraces and enjoys her.

7. Saumya-bandha is the name given by the old poets to a form of congress much in vogue amongst the artful students of the Kamashastra. The wife lies supine, and the husband, as usual, sits;[2] he places both hands under her back, closely embracing her, which she returns by tightly grasping his neck.

8. Jrimbhita-asana. In order to bend the wife's body in the form of a bow, the husband places little pillows or pads beneath her hips and head, he then raises the seat of pleasure and rises to it by kneeling upon a cushion. This is an admirable form of congress, and is greatly enjoyed by both.

9. Veshtita-asana, is when the wife lies upon her back cross-legged,[3] and raises her feet a little; this position is very well fitted for those burning with desire.

10. Venuvidarita is that in which the wife, lying upon her back, places one leg upon her husband's shoulder, and the other on the bed or carpet.

11. Sphutma-uttana-bandha is when the husband, after insertion and penetration, raises the legs of his wife, who

[2] Not as a tailor, but "sitting at squat," upon both feet, somewhat like a bird, a position impossible to Europeans.

[3] Unintelligible without an illustration.

still lies upon her back, and joins her thighs closely together.

Here end the eleven forms of Uttana-bandha; we now proceed to the:

(B) Tiryak (*i.e.*, aslant, awry posture) whose essence consists of the woman lying upon her side. Of this division, there are three sub-divisions:

1. Vinaka-tiryak-bandha is when the husband, placing himself alongside of his wife, raises one of his legs over her hip and leaves the other lying upon the bed or carpet. This A'sana (position) is fitted only for practice upon a grown-up woman; in the case of a younger person, the result is by no means satisfactory.

2. Samputa-tiryak-bandha is when both man and woman lie straight upon their sides, without any movement or change in the position of their limbs.

3. Karkata-tiryak-bandha is when both being upon their sides, the husband lies between his wife's thighs, one under him, and the other being thrown over his flank, a little below the breast.

Here end the three forms of the Tiryak-bandha; and we now proceed to the:

(C) Upavishta (*i.e.*, sitting) posture. Of this division there are ten sub-divisions shown in the figure on the opposite page.

1. Padm-asana. The husband in this favourite position sits cross-legged upon the bed or carpet, and takes his wife upon his lap, placing his hands upon her shoulders.

2. Upapad-asana. In this posture, whilst both are sitting, the woman slightly raises one leg by placing the hand under it, and the husband enjoys her.

3. Vaidhurit-asana. The husband embraces his wife's neck very closely, and she does the same to him.

4. Panipash-asana. The husband holds his wife's feet, and the wife those of her husband.

5. Sanyaman-asana. The husband passes both the legs of his wife under his arms at the elbow, and holds her neck with his hands.

6. Kaurmak-asana (or the tortoise posture). The husband must so sit that his mouth, arms, and legs touch the corresponding members of his wife.

7. Parivartit-asana. In addition to the mutual contact of mouth, arms, and legs, the husband must frequently pass both the legs of his wife under his arms at the elbow.

8. Yugmapad-asana is a name given by the poets to that position in which the husband sits with his legs wide apart, and, after insertion and penetration, presses the thighs of his wife together.

9. Vinarditasana, a form possible only to a very strong man with a very light woman; he raises her by passing both her legs over his arms at the elbow, and moves her about from left to right, but not backwards or forwards, till the supreme moment arrives.

10. Markatasana, is the same position as No. 9; in this, however, the husband moves the wife in a straight line away from his face, that is, backwards and forwards, but not from side to side.

Here end the forms of Upavishta, or sitting-posture. The next is:

(D) Utthita, or the standing posture, which admits of three sub-divisions:

1. Janu-kuru-utthitha-bandha (*i.e.,* "knee and elbow

standing-form"), a posture which also requires great bodily strength in the man. Both stand opposite to each other, and the husband passes his two arms under his wife's knees, supporting her upon the *saignee*, or inner elbow; he then raises her as high as his waist, and enjoys her, whilst she must clasp his neck with both her hands.

2. Hari-vikrama-utthita-bandha; in this form the husband raises only one leg of his wife, who with the other stands upon the ground. It is a position delightful to young women, who thereby soon find themselves *in gloria*.

3. Kirti-utthita-bandha; this requires strength in the man, but not so much as is wanted for the first sub-division. The wife, clasping her hands and placing her legs round her husband's waist, hangs, as it were, to him, whilst he supports her by placing his forearms under her hips.

Here end the forms of Utthita, or standing-posture; and we now come to the:

(E) Vyanta-bandha, which means congress with a woman when she is prone, that is, with the breast and stomach to the bed or carpet. Of this A'sana, there are only two well-known sub-divisions:

1. Dhenuka-vyanta-bandha (the cow-posture):[4] in this position the wife places herself upon all fours, supported on her hands and feet (not her knees), and the husband, approaching from behind, falls upon her waist, and enjoys her as if he were a bull. There is much religious merit in this form.

2. Aybha-vyanta-bandha (or Gajasawa, the elephant

[4] There is nothing of insult in comparison with a cow, which is worshipped by the Hindus.

posture).[5] The wife lies down in such a position that her face, breast, stomach, and thighs all touch the bed or carpet, and the husband, extending himself upon her, and bending himself like an elephant, with the small of the back, much drawn in, works underneath her, and effects insertion.

"O Rajah," said the arch-poet Kalyana Malla, "there are many other forms of congress, such as Harinasana, Sukrasana, Gardhabasana, and so forth; but they are not known to the people, and being useless as well as very difficult of performance, nay, sometimes so full of faults as to be excluded or prohibited, I have, therefore, not related them to you. But if you desire to hear anything more about postures, be pleased to ask, and your servant will attempt to satisfy your curiosity."

"Right well!" exclaimed the king. "I much wish to hear you describe the Purushayitabandha."

"Hear, O Rajah," resumed the poet, "whilst I relate all that requires to be known concerning that form of congress."

Purushayitabandha[6] is the reverse of what men usually practise. In this case the man lies upon his back, draws his wife upon him and enjoys her. It is especially useful when he, being exhausted, is no longer capable of muscular exertion, and when she is ungratified, being still full of the water of love. The wife must, therefore, place

---

[5] The classical idea of elephants, like other retromingents, copulating *a tergo*, was never known to the Hindus, who were too well acquainted with the habits of the animals. It is needless to say that their coition is that of other quadrupeds.

[6] This position is held in great horror by Muslims, who commonly say, "Cursed be he who makes himself earth and woman heaven!"

her husband supine upon the bed or carpet, mount upon his person, and satisfy her desires. Of this form of congress there are three subdivisions:

1. Viparita-bandha, or "contrary position," is when the wife lies straight upon the outstretched person of her husband, her breast being applied to his bosom, presses his waist with her hands, and moving her hips sharply in various directions, enjoys him.

2. Purushayita-bhramara-bandha ("like the large bee"): in this, the wife, having placed her husband at full length upon the bed or carpet, sits at squat upon his thighs, closes her legs firmly after she has effected insertion: and, moving her waist in a circular form, churning, as it were, enjoys her husband, and thoroughly satisfies herself.

3. Utthita-uttana-bandha. The wife, whose passion has not been gratified by previous copulation, should make her husband lie upon his back, and sitting cross-legged upon his thighs, should seize his Linga, effect insertion, and move her waist up and down, advancing and retiring; she will derive great comfort from this process.

Whilst thus reversing the natural order in all these forms of Purushayita, the wife will draw in her breath after the fashion called Sitkara; she will smile gently, and she will show a kind of half shame, making her face so attractive that it cannot well be described. After which she will say to her husband, "O my dear! O thou rogue; this day thou hast come under my control, and hast become subjected to me, being totally defeated in the battle of love!" Her husband manipulates her hair according to art, embraces her and kisses her lower lip; whereupon all her members will relax, she will close her eyes and fall into a swoon of joy.

Moreover, at all times of enjoying Purushayita the wife will remember that without an especial exertion of will on her part, the husband's pleasure will not be perfect. To this end she must ever strive to close and constrict the Yoni until it holds the Linga, as with a finger,[7] opening and shutting at her pleasure, and finally, acting as the hand of the Gopala-girl, who milks the cow. This can be learned only by long practice, and especially by throwing the will into the part to be affected, even as men endeavour to sharpen their hearing,[8] and their sense of touch. While so doing, she will mentally repeat "Kamadeva! Kamadeva," in order that a blessing may rest upon the undertaking. And she will be pleased to hear that the art once learned, is never lost. Her husband will then value her above all women, nor would he exchange her for the most beautiful Rani (queen) in the three worlds. So lovely and pleasant to man is she who constricts.

Let it now be observed that there are sundry kinds

[7] Amongst some races the constrictor vaginæ muscles are abnormally developed. In Abyssinia, for instance, a woman can so exert them as to cause pain to a man, and, when sitting upon his thighs, she can induce the orgasm without moving any other part of her person. Such an artist is called by the Arabs, "Kabbazah," literally meaning "a holder," and it is not surprising that the slave dealers pay large sums for her. All women have more or less the power, but they wholly neglect it; indeed, there are many races in Europe which have never even heard of it. To these the words of wisdom spoken by Kalyana Malla, the poet, should be peculiarly acceptable.

[8] So, it is said, that Orsini, the conspirator, employed the long hours of his captivity in cultivating this sense, until he was able readily to distinguish sounds which other men could not even hear.

and conditions of women whom the wise peremptorily exclude from Purushayita, and the principal exceptions will here be mentioned. First, the Karini-woman. Second, the Harini. Third, she who is pregnant. Fourth, she who has not long left the lying-in chamber. Fifth, a woman of thin and lean body, because the exertion will be too great for her strength. Sixth, a woman suffering from fever or other weakening complaint. Seventh, a virgin; and, eighth, a girl not yet arrived at puberty.

And now having duly concluded the chapter[9] of internal enjoyments, it is good to know that if husband and wife live together in close agreement, as one soul in a single body, they shall be happy in this world, and in that to come. Their good and charitable actions will be an example to mankind, and their peace and harmony will effect their salvation. No one yet has written a book to prevent the separation of the married pair and to show them how they may pass through life in union. Seeing this, I felt compassion, and composed the treatise, offering it to the god Pandurang.

The chief reason for the separation between the married couple and the cause which drives the husband to the embraces of strange women, and the wife to the arms of strange men, is the want of varied pleasures and the monotony which follows possession. There is no doubt about it. Monotony begets satiety, and satiety distaste for congress, especially in one or the other; malicious feelings are engendered, the husband or the wife yield to temptation, and the other follows, being driven by jealousy. For it seldom happens that the two love each

[9] The author, at this place, repeats the signs and symptoms of plenary enjoyment in woman which he gave in Chapter III, Section 3.

other equally, and in exact proportion, therefore is the one more easily seduced by passion than the other. From such separations result polygamy, adulteries, abortions, and every manner of vice, and not only do the erring husband and wife fall into the pit, but they also drag down the names of their deceased ancestors from the place of beatified mortals, either to hell or back again upon this world. Fully understanding the way in which such quarrels arise, I have in this book shown how the husband, by varying the enjoyment of his wife, may live with her as with thirty-two different women, ever varying the enjoyment of her, and rendering satiety impossible. I have also taught all manner of useful arts and mysteries, by which she may render herself pure, beautiful and pleasing in his eyes. Let me, therefore, conclude with the verse of blessing:

"May this treatise,
Ananga ranga, be be-
loved of Man and Woman,
• as long as the Holy River Ganges
springeth from Shiva, with his
wife Gauri on his left side; as long as
Lakshmi loveth Vishnu; as long as
Bramha is engaged in the study
of the Vedas; and as long
as the Earth, the Moon
and the Sun endure."

APPENDIX I

ASTROLOGY IN CONNECTION WITH MARRIAGE[1]

Now is related the effect resulting from the consonance and dissonance, amity and hospitality, between the stars (and destinies) of a couple proposed to be bride and bridegroom.[2] Having ascertained that the houses (*kula*), the family names (*gotra*), and the individual dispositions (*svabhava*) of the postulants are free from inherent blemish,[3] their Gunas (qualities or requisites) must be

[1] We have relegated the astrological and chemical chapters to an appendix. They appear (pp. 120 et seq.) in the Maratha Edit. of the Ananga-Ranga (Bombay, 1842); but it is more than doubtful if they belong to the original work.

[2] As mere children are married in India these precautions and considerations must be taken by the relatives. See the beginning of Chapter VIII.

[3] The fault of families is hereditary ill-repute: the greatest blemish of names is when those of bride and bridegroom exactly correspond, and those of disposition are too well known to require notice.

determined from the zodiacal signs and the asterisms presiding over their birth.[4]

The Gunas, number in total thirty-six, of which at least nineteen are requisite for a prosperous match; and thence upwards, the fruit resulting from their influence is proportional to their number.

Observations upon these subjects will be facilitated by the three following tables:

Table I shows the presiding planet, the genus (or nature) and the caste (in theory not in practice) of the questioner, when the zodiacal sign of his birth-time is known. For instance, if Sol be in Aries at the birth of the patient, his planet is Mars; he belongs to the genus quadruped, and he is by caste a Kshatriya or fighting-man.

TABLE I

Zodiacal Sign	Presiding Planet	Genus	Caste
Aries	Mars	Quadruped	Kshatriya
Taurus	Venus	Quadruped	Vaishya
Gemini	Mercury	Human	Shudra
Cancer	Moon	Insect	Brahman
Leo	Sun	Quadruped	Kshatriya
Virgo	Mercury	Human	Vaishya
Libra	Venus	Human	Shudra
Scorpio	Mras	Insect	Brahman
Sagittarius	Jupiter	Man-horse	Kshatriya
Capricornus	Saturn	Water-man	Vaishya
Aquarius	Saturn	Human	Shudra
Pisces	Jupiter	Aquatic animal	Brahman

[4] The signs and asterisms are set down in the horoscopes, which are drawn up at the child's birth by competent inqu..rers.

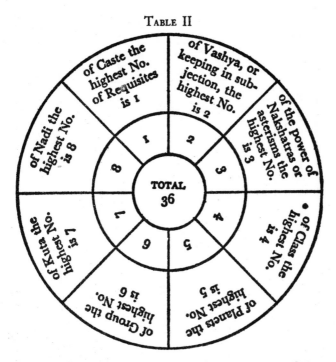

TABLE II

Of Caste the highest No. of Requisites is 1

of Vashya, or keeping in subjection, the highest No. is 2

of the power of Nakshatras or asterisms the highest No. is 3

of Class the highest No. is 4

of Planets the highest No. is 5

of Group the highest No. is 6

of Kuta the highest No. is 7

of Nadi the highest No. is 8

1 2 3 4 5 6 7 8

TOTAL 36

Table II shows the number of Guna, or qualities, requisite for a prosperous match distributed under eight heads.

Table III shows the group and class to which a person belongs when the asterism (Nakshatra, or lunar mansion) of his birth-time is known, together with his Nadi, or hour of twenty-four minutes. The twenty-seven asterisms are classed under three heads: of gods, of men and of demons (Rakshasas), and the asterism determines to which the querent belongs. Moreover, each asterism is divided into four quarters, and of these nine make one

TABLE III

Asterism (Nakshatra)	Group	Class	Nadi. Hour of 24 m	Quarters of Asterisms, showing changes of the Zodiacal Signs.			
				1	2	3	4
Ashvini	God	Horse	First	Cha, 1, i.e. Aries	Che, 1, i.e. do.	Cho, 1, i.e. do.	La, 1, i.e. do.
Bharani	Man	Elephant	Middle	Li, 1, i.e. do.	Lu, 1, i.e. do.	Le, 1, i.e. do.	Lo, 1, i.e. do.
Kritika	Demon	Ram	Last	A, 1, i.e. do.	I, 2, i.e. Taurus	U, 2, i.e. do.	Ve, 2, i.e. do.
Rohini	Man	Serpent	Last	O, 2, i.e. do.	Va, 2, i.e. do.	Vi, 2, i.e. do.	Vu, 2, i.e. do.
Mriga	God	Serpent	Middle	Ve, 2, i.e. do.	Vo, 2, i.e. do.	Ka, 3, i.e. Gemini	Ki, 3, i.e. do.
Ardra	Man	Dog	First	Ku, 3, i.e. do.	Gha, 3, i.e. do.	Na, 3, i.e. do.	Chha, 3, i.e. do.
Punarvasu	God	Cat	First	Ke, 3, i.e. do.	Ko, 3, i.e. do.	Ha, 3, i.e. do.	Hi, 4, i.e. Cancer
Pushya	God	Ram	Middle	Hu, 4, i.e. do.	He, 4, i.e. do.	Ho, 4, i.e. do.	Da, 4, i.e. do.
A'shlesha	Demon	Cat	Last	Di, 4, i.e. do.	Du, 4, i.e. do.	De, 4, i.e. do.	Do, 4, i.e. do.
Magha	Demon	Mouse	Last	Ma, 5, i.e. Leo	Mi, 5, i.e. do.	Mu, 5, i.e. do.	Me, 5, i.e. do.
Purva	Man	Mouse	Middle	Mo, 5, i.e. do.	Ta, 5, i.e. do.	Ti, 5, i.e. do.	Tu, 5, i.e. do.
Uttara	Man	Cow	First	Te, 5, i.e. do.	To, 6, i.e. Virgo	Pa, 6, i.e. do.	Pi, 6, i.e. do.
Hasta	God	Buffalo	First	Pu, 6, i.e. do.	Sha, 6, i.e. do.	Na, 6, i.e. do.	Dha, i.e. do.

Asterism (Nakshatra)	Group	Class	Nadi. Hour of 24 m.	Quarters of Asterism, showing changes of the Zodiacal Signs. 1	2	3	4
Chitra	Demon	Tiger	Middle	Pe, 6, i.e. do.	Po, 6, i.e. do.	Ra, 7, i.e. Libra	Ri, 7, i.e. do.
Svati	God	Buffalo	Last	Ru, 7, i.e. do.	Re, 7, i.e. do.	Ro, 7, i.e. do.	La, 7, i.e. do.
Vishakha	Demon	Tiger	Last	Zi, 7, i.e. do.	Zu, 7, i.e. do.	Ze, 7, i.e. do.	Zo, 8, i.e. Scorpio
Anuradha	God	Deer	Middle	Na, 8, i.e. do.	Ni, 8, i.e. do.	Nu, 8, i.e. do.	Ne, 8, i.e. do.
Jyeshtha	Demon	Deer	First	No, 8, i.e. do	Ya, 8, i.e. do.	Yi, 8, i.e. do.	Yu, 8, i.e. do.
Mula	Demon	Dog	First	Ye, 9, i.e. Sagittarius	Yo, 9, i.e. do.	Bha, 9, i.e. do.	Bhi, 9, i.e. do.
Purvashadha	Man	Monkey	Middle	Bhu, 9, i.e. do.	Dha, 9, i.e. do.	Pha, 9, i.e. do.	Dha, 9, i.e. do.
Uttarashadha	Man	Ichneumon	Last	Bhe, 9, i.e. do.	Bho, 10, i.e. Capricornus	Ga, 10, i.e. do.	Gi, 10, i.e. do.
Shravana	God	Monkey	Last	Khi, 10, i.e. do.	Khu, 10, i.e. do.	Khe, 10, i.e. do.	Kho, 10, i.e. do.
Dhanishtha	Demon	Lion	Middle	Ga, 10, i.e. do.	Gi, 10, i.e. do.	Gu, 11, i.e. Aquarius	Ge, 11, i.e. do.
Shatataraka	Demon	Horse	First	Go, 11, i.e. do.	Sa, 11, i.e. do.	Si, 11, i.e. do.	Su, 11, i.e. do.
Purvabhadra-pada	Man	Lion	First	Se, 11, i.e. do.	So, 11, i.e. do.	Da, 11, i.e. do.	Di, 12, i.e. Pisces
Uttarabhadra-pada	Man	Cow	Middle	Du, 12, i.e. do.	Zam, 12, i.e. do.	N, 12, i.e. do.	Yo, 12, i.e. do.
Retati	God	Elephant	Last	Do, 12, i.e. do.	Do, 12, i.e. do.	Cha, 12, i.e. do.	Chi, 12, i.e. do.

zodiacal sign. The name-letter used in last quarter stands for that quarter.

And now to consider the tables more carefully. As is shown by No. II, the Gunas are of various values, and are distributed under eight heads.

1. Caste. If both be of the same, or the caste of the bridegroom be higher, there is one Guna (of the thirty-six) otherwise there is none.

2. Vashya, or keeping in subjection, one of the prime considerations of marriage. If the zodiacal signs of bride and bridegroom be of the same genus (Table I) this represents two Gunas. If the person kept in subjection be also the "food" of the other, this counts for only one-half (Guna). If there be natural friendship between the genera of the bride and bridegroom this stands for two Gunas; and if one be an enemy to the other, and also keep the other in subjection, it represents only one Guna. The consideration is as follows: To the human genus every quadruped, saving only the lion, remains in subjection; for instance, the quadruped ram is subject to, and is the "food" of, the human genus, with one exception, the Brahman. The same is the case with the fish and the crab amongst lower animals. The scorpion is the general enemy to the human race, and other animals are enemies as well as food. Thus we discover which of the two persons will hold the other in subjection.

3. The Nakshatras (Table III) must be considered as follows: The bride's asterism should be counted from that of the bridegroom, and the number be divided by nine. If the remainder be three, five or seven, it is a sign of bad fortune; and *vice versa* with all others. Similarly

the bridegroom's lunation should be counted from the bride's; and if, after dividing as before by nine, the remainders of both parties indicate good fortune, this counts as three Gunas, the maximum. Only if one portend well, it counts as one Guna and a half: otherwise there is no Guna.

4. Class. Perfect friendship counts for four Gunas; common friendship as three, indifference as two; enmity as one, an exceeding enmity as half a Guna. Perfect friendship can subsist only between two human beings of the same caste. Cows and buffaloes, elephants and rams, live in common friendship. Cows and tigers, horses and buffaloes, lions and elephants, rams and monkeys, dogs and deer, cats and mice, snakes and ichneumons are exceedingly inimical. Common enmity and indifference are easily exemplified by the lives of ordinary men and beasts.

5. Planets. If the presiding planets of both persons be the same, and there be perfect friendship, this counts for five Gunas; or four if only common friendship. If there be friendship with an enemy of the other person it reduces the value to one Guna, and if both have such friendship to one half. In cases of mutual indifference the Gunas amount to three, and if there be mutual enmity there is no Guna.

6. Groups as in Table III. If both belong to the same group, six Gunas are present; also if the bridegroom belong to the god-group and the bride to the man-group. The reverse reduces it five: if the bridegroom be of demon-group, and the bride of god-group, there is only one Guna, and in all other cases none.

7. Kuta, that is the agreement of the zodiacal signs and asterisms of bride and bridegroom. It is of two kinds, auspicious and ill-omened. The Kuta is fortunate if the bride and bridegroom be born in the same sign, but in different asterisms, or in the same asterisms, but in different signs, or, lastly, in the same asterisms but in different quarters. A difference of seven asterisms is also auspicious; for instance, if the bridegroom's asterism be Ashvini (Table III), and that of the bride Pushya. The same is the case with three, four, ten and eleven asterisms, and with a second sign from an even sign; for instance, Cancer being the fourth is an even sign, and if the sign of one party be Cancer and the other Virgo, the Kuta is auspicious. This is also the case with a sixth sign from an even sign; and an eighth and a twelfth from an odd sign. But a second sign, a fifth, a sixth, a ninth, and a twelfth from an odd sign, and an eighth from an even sign, are unfortunate Kutas. The Gunas of Leo and Virgo are both auspicious. If there be a fortunate Kuta, and the sign of the bridegroom be remote from that of the bride, and if there be enmity between the classes of the two, this conjunction will represent six Gunas. If there be the same sign and different asterisms, or the same asterism and different signs, the Gunas number five. In an unfortunate Kuta if there be friendship between the classes of the postulants, and the bride's asterism be remote from that of the bridegroom this counts for four Gunas; but if there be only a single condition, it reduces the requisites to one. In all other cases there is no Kuta.

8. The Nadi or point of time. If the Nadis of the

bride and bridegroom be different, as *e.g.*, first and last, first and middle, last and middle, this conjunction represents eight Gunas. The requisites are nil when the Nadi is the same.

APPENDIX II

Now is related the Rasayana, or preparation of metals for medicinal purposes.

First Recipe

For the curing of disease caused by quicksilver.[1] Take sixty-four Tolas (each three drachms) of the juice of betel-plant (*piper betel*); mix with equal quantities of the juice of Bhringaraja (*eclipta postrata*), juice of the Tulsi (*ocymum basilicum*, herb basil) and goat's milk; and rub the mixture into all parts of the body for two days, each day two pahars (six hours) followed by a cold bath.

[1] The Hindus are supposed to have introduced the internal use of mercury which, in the shape of corrosive sublimate, found its way to Europe. They must have soon discovered the hideous effects of its abuse: in countries like Central Africa, where mercury is unknown, Syphilis never attacks the bones of the nose or face. The remedy in the text can do neither good nor harm.

Second Recipe

For reducing mercury to Bhasma (ashes, metallic oxide). Take of purified quicksilver and sulphur equal parts, and levigate with the sap of the Banyan-tree (*ficus indica*); place the preparation in an earthen pot over a slow fire and stir with a stick of the Banyan-tree for a whole day. If two Gunjas (1 5/10 grs. troy) of this medicine be eaten at early morning in betel leaf, digestion is improved and the powers of copulation are increased.

Third Recipe

For preparing Hemagarbha, the Elixir Vitæ which contains gold. Take three parts of purified quicksilver; one part and a half of sulphur; one part of gold; two parts of the ashes (metallic oxide) of copper and calx of pearls and coral, each one-tenth of a part. Levigate in a mortar for seven days with the juice of the Kumari (*aloe perfoliata*), make into a ball, cover well with a piece of cotton cloth and place in an earthen vessel, containing a little sulphur: the mouth must be well closed, leaving for the escape of smoke a small hole which must be kept open with a needle if necessary. Set the vessel over a Valukayantra (bain marie, or sandbath) under which a slow fire is kindled. After about half a Ghataka (12 minutes) the fire must be diminished and allowed to extinguish. Remove the ball and use as the doctor directs.

Fourth Recipe

For reducing Harital (Sanskrit, hartalaka, sulphuret of arsenic, yellow orpiment) to ashes, or metallic oxide.

Levigate yellow orpiment and knead it with the juice of the plant Nagar-juni (a Cyperus grass). Levigate again with the juice of the Pinpalli (*piper longum*) and the Piper betel for two days. Make balls of the preparation; dry in shade; then set in earthen vessel in a *bain marie*. A hot fire must be kept up till the orpiment is thoroughly "cooked", and allow the fire to diminish and extinguish. Lastly, remove the balls from the vessel and use in every disease.

Fifth Recipe

For absorbing all other metals by purified mercury. Thoroughly levigate quicksilver with the juice of the "seven minor poisons", *viz.*, Arka (*Callotropis gigantea*), Sehunda (*Euphorbia*), Dhatura (*Stramonium*, white thorn-apple), Langali (*Jussiaea repens*), Karavira (oleander) or Soma[2] and opium. By this means mercury loses its wings and cannot fly, while it gets a mouth and eats up every metal with speed.

Sixth Recipe

A sovereign remedy against all diseases and death. Take Abhraka (tale) and levigate with the milky sap of the Arka for the space of a day. Then wrap up the preparation in Arka-leaves and boil in a heap of Gobar (cow-dung) cakes about two feet thick. Repeat this boiling with fresh leaves for seven times, then infuse the preparation three times in a decoction of Parambi Marathi, the fibrous roots of the Banyan-tree. In this way the

[2] So the Dictionaries, naming very different plants, Nerium odorum (with poisonous root) and the harmless holy Soma (*Sercostamma*). But Kara-vira is a word of many meanings.

mineral is "killed"; its impurities are removed and it becomes nishchandra talc. Boil equal parts of this and Ghi (clarified butter) in an iron vessel till the butter is absorbed, and it is ready for use; it cures every complaint, including old age and death.

Some Titles On
HINDUISM
from PILGRIMS PUBLISHING

**PILGRIMS
BOOK HOUSE**

For Catalog and more Information Mail or Fax to:

PILGRIMS BOOK HOUSE
Mail Order, P.O.Box 3872, Kathmandu, Nepal
Tel: 977-1-424942   Fax: 977-1-424943
e-mail: mailorder@pilgrims.wlink.com.np
website : www.pilgrimsbooks.com